James Pycroft

Oxford Memories

A Retrospect After Fifty Years

James Pycroft

Oxford Memories

A Retrospect After Fifty Years

ISBN/EAN: 9783744689632

Printed in Europe, USA, Canada, Australia, Japan

Cover: Foto ©ninafisch / pixelio.de

More available books at **www.hansebooks.com**

OXFORD MEMORIES

A RETROSPECT

AFTER FIFTY YEARS

BY THE REV.

JAMES PYCROFT B.A.

TRINITY COLLEGE OXFORD

IN TWO VOLUMES.

VOL. II.

LONDON
RICHARD BENTLEY & SON, NEW BURLINGTON STREET
Publishers in Ordinary to Her Majesty the Queen
1886

[The right of translation and all other rights reserved.]

CONTENTS.

CHAP.	PAGE
XV.—COMMEMORATION "ROWS" AND OTHER "ROWS" BETWEEN "TOWN" AND "GOWN"	1
XVI.—THE TRACTARIAN PARTY	23
XVII.—WILD OATS AND A SAD CROP	33
XVIII.—PAST RECOVERY	44
XIX.—TRUE TO THE DEATH	54
XX.—AQUATICS—A TALE OF WOE	70
XXI.—CRICKET OF FIFTY YEARS SINCE	84
XXII.—BOWLING, PAST AND PRESENT—REMINISCENCES	106
XXIII.—FELIX, MYNN, COBBETT, AND OTHER VETERANS	125
XXIV.—THE OLD KENT ELEVEN	166
XXV.—REFLECTIONS AT "LORD'S"	189
XXVI.—A TALE OF RUSTICATION	211
XXVII.—A TALE OF RUSTICATION CONTINUED	219
XXVIII.—A SURVEY OF UNIVERSITY ADVANTAGES	233
XXIX.—INFLUENCES, SOCIAL AND LOCAL, AT OXFORD	249
XXX.—GETTING OUR SONS OFF OUR HANDS	263
XXXI.—THE GOOD OLD TIMES—PAST AND PRESENT COMPARED	287

OXFORD MEMORIES.

CHAPTER XV.

COMMEMORATION "ROWS" AND OTHER "ROWS" BETWEEN "TOWN" AND "GOWN."

As to the commemoration rows, a few years since they had become a disgrace and the theatre a perfect bear garden. This was not so in my time. Jokes and sentiments of a personal nature used to be heard with rather noisy notes of approbation, but nothing to complain of. Names of distinguished men were called out for applause or hisses. Once "the Forty Pros" (pro-proctors chosen for the occasion) were followed by "the Forty Thieves," and when Travers Twiss was profuse in his Latin superlatives, *fortissimus et doctissimus* was followed with a suggestion of "et Travers Twissimus." It was in later times when Mr. Mitchell, as Public Orator, with a very port-wine complexion, came to a pause, some one shouted, "Take a glass of water," which provoked the reply, " He doesn't know the taste of it." But then society in Oxford, as elsewhere, was less mixed and Oxford men were more amenable to the laws of good taste and propriety.

At Cambridge I was surprised to hear that this practice was as bad, or worse, and the following was adduced as a specimen of what had happened or might happen at any time :

Dr. Whewell, though one of the foremost men of science of his day, was saluted with :

" Billy, take your hat off."

No notice.

" Billy, why don't you take off that 'shocking bad hat'?" As still no notice was taken, there was an uproar, and three cheers and hisses for Billy. At length, as the gallery seemed quite resolved to stop all the proceedings till obeyed, some one spoke to the doctor, and off came the obnoxious hat.

" Now three cheers for our noble selves."

Shouts of triumph and of victory followed this proposal.

" Now, Billy, after this you'll know how to behave yourself another time."

Sad! sad! that such conduct should prevail in such a place, with so little reverence for either age or worth.

At the commemoration in 1843 the Junior Proctor had made himself so unpopular that the theatre rang with loud and continual notes of disapprobation. This was carried to a disgraceful éxtent in manner and duration. After one burst of applause for the Vice-Chancellor, Dr. Wynter, one continued storm of yelling and hissing was kept up by the rioters. The honorary degrees, only two, were conferred in dumb show. The "Creweian Oration," by the Professor of Poetry, Mr. Garbett, was read, but not a word could be heard. Tired out and disgusted, as was every one else not in the "yelling gallery," the Vice-Chancellor dissolved the convocation, the prize poems and essays being left without recital!

The most noticeable Commemoration, with the installation of the Duke of Wellington, I remember exactly as it is described by Wilson Croker in a letter to his wife:

"Before the business in the theatre opened, the young men in the galleries amused themselves by calling out and hooting, 'Lord Brougham,' 'Lord Grey and his cousins,' and 'The Whigs and pickpockets,' and so forth, enacting quite what the Romans called *saturnalia*. The protestations were less noisy till they came to Lord Encombe. When after shaking hands with the Lord Chancellor, Lord

Encombe went up and shook hands with his old grandfather, Lord Eldon, and when, the seats being full, he sat down at his feet, the applause was astounding. Then there was such a crush in the area that one poor little boy was nearly stifled till some of the doctors leaned over and pulled him up into their seats. This caused the duke to interfere, and to show them how to place themselves properly and to make room. Then began recitations, Greek, Latin, and English, and some good verses by Mr. Arnould (the present Sir Joshua) on the Hospice of St. Bernard, and when, after alluding to Bonaparte's passage of the Alps, he came to the lines about him whom

"'—— A world could not subdue,
Bent to thy prowess, chief of Waterloo!'

such was the enthusiasm the people seemed to go mad. The whole assembly started up; the ladies and the grave semicircle of doctors became as much excited as the boys in the gallery—such peals of shouting, such waving of handkerchiefs and caps, such extravagant clapping and stamping till the air became one cloud of dust! During all this the duke sat like a statue; at last he took some notice, took off his cap lightly, and pointed to the reciter to go on."

Isaac Williams remarked to me afterwards, "Those lines for a clap-trap were an after-thought. I had inquired and found the prize poem had originally nothing of the kind." The author was Mr. Arnould, of Wadham College, afterwards Sir Joshua Arnould, Chief Justice of Bombay.

Adverting to Mr. Dyer's case, the one danger the dons feared was the renewal of the old Town and Gown rows, then for some few years out of date. At Cambridge Town and Gown rows lasted rather longer than at Oxford. There is in "Verdant Green," an exaggerated account of a story which I once wrote, but the true version as I heard it, not long after the event, from my friend the late Rev. Henry Corrance, who was a principal actor in the scene, is worth repeating in a more durable form:

Just before the 5th of November, the usual time for Town and Gown fights, some of the leaders of the fray on the University side reflected that it seemed rather unworthy of Cantab prowess that year after year one Bill Spinks should be able to stand forth and to defy the host, and to say, " Send out your best fellow to meet me, man to man." As Homer said of the challenge of Ajax, " They were all afraid to accept the challenge and ashamed to refuse it." So they subscribed for the expenses and sent for Peter Crawley. Peter had been the champion of England, and had beaten Jem Ward; though Jem told my friend Fred Gale (*quis nescit Fred Gale?*) it was a fluke. He had intended, when all seemed in his favour, to receive one and return three as scientific counter-hits, and thus to hit Peter out of time, but unluckily the one received took Jem on the temple, and that turned the fortune of the day. This was almost the dying speech and confession of James Ward, artist as well as ex-prize-fighter, at the Victuallers' Asylum, where, not long since, he ended his days. No wonder, therefore, Peter Crawley seemed the right man for the occasion. *Dolus an virtus quis in hoste requirit*; or, as Paddy said, "If only we can bate 'em we need not be particular." So on the eventful evening Peter Crawley, in Trinity cap and gown, attended by Corrance, a strong fellow of good twelve stone, sallied out at the head of the Trinity men. They soon found Bill Spinks and his party ready for a triumph.

First of all one party stood on one side of the arena and the other party on the other side; and what seems to prove how true are all Homer's battles to real life, speeches were made on both sides to begin with; ay, not only speeches but Homeric speeches too; for our poet's ἔπ εα πτερόεντα, *winged words* have never been as well illustrated by any commentator as they were on the occasion I am to describe. For there were no long prosy speeches with a beginning, middle and end to them, all about the example of our forefathers, the interests of ourselves, and the good opinion of posterity; but by *winged words* I understand short, pithy, pointed sentences like the following, which we can almost fancy that we see as they fly like winged arrows shot and returned from opposing ranks, and very readily suggest as an apt interpretation the modern term "chaff."

"You're afeard" (afraid), cried the one party.

When full time had been allowed to show that this missile fell harmless from their callous breasts, it was handed back with

"You're another," retort courteous.

Then again the assailants tried a second shot, aimed personally and directly at Peter Crawley himself, but all in vain; it did not stagger him in the least. We will not give the common vernacular, but render it classically and in Johnsonese, as Macaulay terms it:

"I'll obfuscate your luminaries, Master Trinity."

"Who cares for a sanguineous plebeian!" replied the counterfeit collegian.

So far it was mere skirmishing at a distance, but

presently the two champions advanced into the space between, where, after playing with Mr. William Spinks by a little sparring, Peter let out right and left, laying his enemy on the ground. Then the fight became general for a few minutes, when suddenly a cry was raised, " To the rescue ! " and behold, at a little distance, a proctor, Mr. Musgrave, late Bishop of Hereford, was seen with his gown torn and so buffeted and rushed against as to be in some personal danger. This was quickly seen by my friend Corrance, who being himself none of the weakest, and being closely followed by his man-of-arms, brought up timely succour. Quickly they were at the embryo prelate's side ; and as Peter Crawley was now upon his mettle, and found that his prowess could be exerted with advantage, he put it forth to some purpose ; and as the rescued dignitary saw his assailants fall right and left before Peter Crawley's potent arm, doubtless he felt like the Duke of Wellington when joined by Blucher at Waterloo ; and as soon as his much-poked ribs, recovering from their forcible compression, gave him breath to speak, catching hold of Corrance's shoulder from behind, he exclaimed, " A wonderfully fine young man with his fists that. Who is he, pray ? I wish particularly to know."

Whether Peter Crawley ever afterwards applied to his lordship for church patronage for any of his kith or kin for the good and useful service that day done I cannot tell, but if he has not, either from diffidence or magnanimity, all bishops will allow that the said Peter Crawley has evinced a degree of consideration and modesty rarely found among gentlemen of a higher class.

But the Oxford Town and Gown rows dated from a period six centuries back. Matthew Paris records riots caused by the jealousy of the citizens of Oxford against the students as early as A.D. 1240, when the students had the worst of the fray, and were obliged to retire from the city, and on one occasion to take refuge at Northampton and on another at Stamford. This is the more remarkable, because the students then were probably far more numerous than at present; there were many foreigners from Paris and other cities of the Continent. In the time of the founder of Merton they were estimated at fifteen thousand. This is incredible; let us believe a very large number.

In the days of St. Scholastica the Virgin, February 10, 1354, an affray took place which cost many lives. The Bishop of Lincoln, in whose diocese Oxford then was, placed the townsmen under an interdict, from which they were only released on condition that the commonalty of Oxford should celebrate an anniversary in St. Mary's church for the souls of the clerks and others killed in the conflict, when the gutter of Brewer's or Slaughter Lane ran with academic blood. As late as 1825, in which year the citizens were first released by Convocation, they used to make offerings just after the Litany to the number of sixty-three, the number of the slain. Mr. Short said, while this old indignity lasted we used to ask the leading citizens to dinner, and so smoothed it off and made the best of it. Originally the sixty-three had to attend with ropes round their necks.

At the time of the later Town and Gown rows young men were in other ways more of a physical force and rowdy character, and the old Tom-and-Jerry practices were too much in fashion. The late Marquis of Waterford was very popular, and his pranks from about 1830-1840 betrayed not a few young men into the same practical jokes and sometimes serious scrapes. At Oxford, as at other places, it commonly took the form of wrenching off knockers and dragging out the handles of door-bells. Mr. Cox says: "My fine old brass knocker in Merton Street was a special object of desire and attack. Several times late in the evening had I rescued it just in time on hearing the grating sound of a bar or poker." Christchurch fountain, on being cleared out, was found floored with knockers, ornaments, devices, sign-boards, &c. But the proctor pounced on some, and made the detected pay for a whole lot of knockers abstracted by others as well as by themselves, and some rustications followed the offence. These frolics were a remnant of what was far more easy in the days of the old watchmen—the old "Charlies"—than in the days of the "Peelers"—the new police, the introduction of Sir Robert Peel.

The marquis, when hunting in Leicestershire, abstracted sign-boards and played tricks of various kinds, which at last met with notice from the magistrates. I know nothing more shocking than when any practical joke ends in a fatal accident, as happened to one young man while playing "Waterford tricks" near Leicester. A nephew of Sir Vere Isham upset one of the iron eagles from the gate-post of his uncle's park, and fell with it to the ground; the tip of one wing pierced his side, and he died the next day. I one day was sculling near the Cherwell when one man in a sharp-beaked Thames wherry rowed as a joke across another who had hardly ever been in a boat before, and who therefore proved unable to defend himself. I shouted a warning ; the sharp point painfully grazed his ribs, and by a few more inches it would have crushed into his body !

Mr. Bedell Cox tells us of a poetical tribute to the memory of Lord Stowell, the eminent jurisconsult, brother of Lord Eldon, who died in 1836 :—

> "Ossa quieta, precor, tutâ requiescite urnâ,
> Ut sit humus cineri non onerosa tuo."

Whether or not that prayer was granted as to the urn, to his bones and ashes, I know not. But now we have in Oxford not only *Ossa* but *Pelion*, in the shape of his and his brother's colossal statues by Nelson, which are deposited in the splendid and useful library of University College, set up at the expense of the noble family as a kind of mausoleum in honour of the two great brothers.

Cox also gives us a more witty quotation when he speaks of an annual sum from the University Press—" What a famous milch cow that press :

> 'Fontes perpetues ubera *pressa* dabunt.'"

Mr. Cox records various criticisms about proctors.

Laudatur ab his is not new. When Mr. Dale, a big man, who was hooted, ended his year of office with little Mr. Laud, he was said to have discharged his office "*cum parvâ Laude.*"

Some years before, Mr. Marshall, of Balliol College, on Commemoration Day, on retiring from the theatre, was struck in the face with an orange thrown at him from the gallery. The offender was not discovered:

"In certum, qua pulsa manu, quo turbine adacta
Nec se (Marshalle) jactavit vulnere quisquam."

Among the proctors there have been distinguished names. Copleston, Rigaud, Shuttleworth, Hussey, Symons, Lightfoot, Longley and Liddell could all date some event from *me Procuratore.*

The old derivation of the term among undergraduates was not *pro* and *curo*, but from *pro* for and *curro* to run—that is, to run for, to catch a man. The attendant on the proctors, in my time called the Marshal, had proved too fleet of foot for most of those who replied, as was said, to the challenge, "*Siste, per fidem*" by "*Curre, per Jovem.*" About 1830 a "University Police" was established, which relieved the proctors of much disagreeable work; still some men refused the office of proctor, not liking the night work, searching houses of ill-fame, and sometimes hunting up and even running down those unfortunates whom Proctor Ellerton called *pestes noctivagæ,* "the pestilence which walketh in darkness." John Sparkes, one of the old professional cricketers, told me he used to attend on proctors sometimes in place of the marshal, and from all sorts of queer hiding-places he would hear a whisper — "Pray, Sparkes, don't split on me." I could have told the proctor which side Sparkes would take, especially if the offender was one of the cricket eleven.

Antony Wood shows us that tricks on freshmen were known in his day—some two hundred years ago. The freshman was seated in hall; every one around was required to make a jest or say some clever nonsense. If the freshman made a dull speech, they would "chuck" him, or with sharp nail give him a rude chuck under the chin. Then came a scene: the cook made pots of "caudle" at his charge, his share of the caudle to be salted if he did not, as usual, pluck off his gown and band and affect the low fellow, and make an amusing speech. These speeches were rarely as good probably as the following specimen by Antony Wood:

"Most Reverend Seniors,—May it please your

gravities to admit into your presence a kitten of the Muses, and a mere frog of Helicon, to croak the cataracts of his plumbeous cerebrosity before your sagacious ingenuities. Expect not that I should thunder out demi-cannon words. I will not sublimate nor tonitruate sounds, for my Hippocrene is at the lowest ebb, nor will my brains evaporate into high hyperboles. I have not yet been fed with the pap of Aristotle, nor even sucked the dugs of Alma Mater."

From the following strain in which Wood continues, it seems that men "read for the pot" even in those days: "I am not one of the University bloodhounds that seek for preferment, their noses as acute as their ears, that lie *perdu* for places. These are they who esteem a tavern as bad as purgatory, and wine more superstitious than holy water."

The "Oxford Sausage," also published in the middle of the last century, shows much of the manners and customs of the day. Blagrave, like old John Sheard, was the job master; Glass and Nourse were the surgeons, like Tuckwell and Ogle of my time; Ben Tyrrell, the confectioner, was the Jupper of the day; and Nell Bachelor, like old Mother Fletcher, was the pie woman, all familiar names of *Universitas*. Nell Bachelor is immortalized also by the following epitaph from "Oxoniana":

> "Here deep in the dust,
>   The mouldy old crust,
>   Of Nell Bachelor lately was shoven,
>   Who was skilled in the arts
>   Of pies, puddings, and tarts,
>   And knew every use of the oven.
>
>   When she'd lived long enough,
>   She made her last puff—
>   A puff by her husband much praised;
>   Now here she doth lie,
>   To make a dirt pie,
>   In hopes that her dust will be raised."

Anything like rough play in my time to compare with Antony Wood's experience was almost unknown, though the Æsthetics lately provoked it. There was nothing like æstheticism in my day at Oxford. One class of men used to read; the others to shoot, hunt, or row. Even music and drawing were rare as resources in college. Athleticism stood in the place of æstheticism; even the word would have puzzled us. The temper of the times inclined rather to the manly than to the effeminate; though, while aware of the excess to which a love of china or sun-flowers may be carried, I can only greet such expressions of refinement as a taste well suited to qualify the roughness of days gone by.

Excess works its own cure, exciting a spirit against it. So, about ten years since, there was a disturbance at Oxford which was circulated far and wide in the daily papers.

A young æsthete had his room wrecked. His furniture and his china, his peacock feathers and his other tomfooleries had been reduced to ruin. It is urged on the other hand that he had so far forgotten himself as to speak disrespectfully of the college boat, and that his punishment was justly deserved. "The controversy," says a writer of the day, "is a very pretty one and up to this moment it is being most acrimoniously carried on, and on the whole the oarsmen, blunt and soldier-like as is their diction, are getting the best of the dispute. The Æsthetes abuse them as Bœotians, and call them brutal, stupid, and ill-educated. To this the Athletes reply, with some promptitude, that there are more boating men to be found in the First class than any furnished by the æsthetic contingent, and one of their number goes so far as to make a very uncomplimentary remark of another kind. The sarcasm is one upon which we need not dwell, but it seems that the Æsthetes have gone rather out of their way to provoke it. Amidst all the coarseness and roughness of Oxford there runs a wholesome and manly dislike of everything that is sickly, mean, and effeminate, and there is also a tendency to associate effeminacy with other failings. The suspicion is on the whole not unfounded, and young men who are fond of feathers, fans, and crockery had perhaps better seek some other place than an Oxford college for the gratification of their peculiar tastes."

It is too little considered that in early times our churches were made use of for secular as well as for religious purposes. Even after the Reformation, which did much to abolish this social use of churches, the Cantabs acted their " Aularia of Plautus" in King's Chapel, converted into a theatre, before Queen Elizabeth. Her Majesty attended service in the morning with Dr. Perore's Latin sermon, and the theatricals in the same place in the evening.

"Before this," says Jeffreason, "churches were places of promenade and jollity, also for warehouses for the farmers' sacks and the merchants' wares, to be safe in days of rapine from thieves and marauders. In short, the nave of the church was the common hall for all public business. Such buildings were too useful and too scarce to be reserved only for Sundays."

Since it is well known that in mediæval days in

the nave of a church you might see the farmer's sacks left while service was done in the chancel, we cannot be surprised to hear that college exercises and celebrations were performed at St. Mary's before Archbishop Sheldon in 1664 instructed Sir Christopher Wren to build the Sheldonian Theatre. Strange to say, Evelyn informs us that though Dr. Sheldon had spent £25,000 on the work, it was never seen by its benefactor—" my Lord Archbishop told me he never did or ever would see it."

Samuel Pepys tells us in his Diary how in 1668 he saw the theatre almost completed, and how high the fees were for the sights of Oxford in those days. " We came to Oxford, a very sweet place, and paid our guide £1 2s. 6d.; the boy that showed us over the college, 1s." This was reasonable, but we find " to him that showed us the schools and library, 10s.; to him that showed us All Souls and Chichley's picture, 5s.; bottle of sack, 1s. Oxford mighty fine place, and well seated, and cheap entertainment. At night came to Abingdon, where had been a fair, and met many people and scholars coming home; some pretty good musick, and sang and danced till supper, 5s."

The theatre was five years in building, and on

the 9th July, 1685, was a grand opening, described by Evelyn: "The dedication was with the greatest splendour and formality, and drew a crowd of strangers from all parts of the nation. Dr. South, the University's orator, made an eloquent speech, and not without some malicious and indecent reflections on the Royal Society. But to let that pass from an ill-natured man: the rest was in praise of the Archbishop and the ingenious architect. This ended with loud musick and panegyric speeches, and the next day with the more solemn lectures in all the faculties."

There seems to have been some one even then to represent the folly and the insolence that has disgraced the gallery at commemorations at the present day. This was the *Terræ filius*, the University jester, "who entertained the auditory with a tedious, abusive rhapsody most unbecoming the gravity of the University, so that unless it be suppressed it will be of ill consequence, as I afterwards," said Evelyn, "expressed my sense of it to the Vice-Chancellor and several heads of houses, who were perfectly ashamed of it, and resolved to take care of it in future."—Still it was twenty years before the office of Terræ Filius was suppressed.

"He was appointed," says Jeffreason, "as an

academic Merry Andrew." There were generally two, who worked in couples and talked up to each other with pre-arranged jests. Speeches being in Latin, and unintelligible to the majority, these jesters were engaged to enliven the proceedings. The jester might interpose ridiculous comments and would indulge in satire. Sometimes he carried it too far. One was deprived of his fellowship at New College. Imagine a *Terræ filius* speech, written by Dr. South, who held this queer office, preserved in the Bodleian, "very deficient in wit and its topics low and vulgar!" Commemorations and *encœnia*, begun with the Earl of Westmorland's installation in 1759, were commenced with a caution significant of the rowdy manners of commemorations since, *that the students behave with such order and decency as become gentlemen of a liberal education.* At first it was a tedious business of eight hours. No wonder men sought relief in fun of any kind. At the installation of the Duke of Portland in 1793, luckily the ladies were admitted first; for a rush of 3,000 men was made. Gowns were torn, caps broken, and pugilistic rounds fought. The "Broad" was strewn with shoes, buckles, gowns, caps and prostrate men. Pick-pockets from town came dressed in M.A. costume. Fancy all this row when Mrs. Billington sang, as Catalani did in 1810 and Jenny Lind on a recent occasion. Again in 1818 an eye-witness writes: "At nine o'clock the outer gates were opened, when, even ladies had their clothes torn to rags, and lost shoes, trinkets, &c. Numbers of trinkets were afterwards picked from the mud.

In a comedy called "The Act at Oxford," at Drury Lane, 1704, a *Terræ filius* is introduced, who thus introduces himself and his vocation:

"To begin, I will first acquaint you with what a *Terræ filius* is. Why, he's the University jester, the terror of fuddling doctors and dissolute commoners, a servitor in scandal and harlequin of the sciences. His continual railing at the University looks as if he were married to her, and his expulsion proves that he is divorced from her."

CHAPTER XVI.

THE TRACTARIAN PARTY.

The Tractarian party was now forming with Keble, Pusey, Isaac Williams, Newman, and others—a party which aspired to promote greater reverence for holy places, a wonderful renovation and increase of churches, and also a purpose and a party for certain earnest-minded men who had heretofore found little sympathy but with Evangelicals or Dissenters. But, on the other hand, their writers seemed to be working the problem of how near men could go to the Popish candle without singeing their wings. About a hundred "perverts" were soon reckoned and duly honoured with notices in the public prints, and with far more notoriety than most of them would otherwise have achieved, and not a few, after preaching Tractarianism as the very antidote to Popery, ended by being infected by that very complaint.

The " Tracts " became bolder and bolder, till at

last Newman, with "Tract 90," drew down a resolution from the Hebdomadal Board—," That such modes of interpretation, evading rather than explaining the sense of the Thirty-nine Articles, and reconciling subscription to them with the adoption of errors they were designed to counteract, are inconsistent with the Statutes of the University, which require subscription to the Articles and the instruction of students in them."

Newman was soon followed by Mr. Sibthorpe, Fellow of Magdalen, with a very Popish sermon. But Sibthorpe soon found out his error, and returned to the Anglican Church. He was a man very much respected as sincere but impressionable.

Without questioning the sincerity of these hundred or more perverts, men act from mixed motives, and are swayed by influences from without. There is another kind of infection besides the physical. A panic will exemplify how one man catches strong emotions from the many. It is very notable also that perversion declined when no longer a notoriety, where less distinction or celebrity attached to it. A little later, going to Rome created as little public interest as going to Romford, and there is no doubt that what ceased to be original, and ceased to add distinction, lost much of its attraction.

Then came the Macmullen controversy. Aware

of his Romish tendencies, Dr. Hampden would not allow Macmullen, of Corpus College, on taking his B.D. degree to argue (*pro formâ*) on subjects of his own choice, but ingeniously set this test thesis—" The Church of England does not teach, nor can it be proved from Scripture, that any change takes place in the elements by consecration." There was much litigation, but Macmullen succeeded in refusing this test thesis. The truth was, Hampden was endeavouring to make what had long been a mere formal exercise a test of doctrine, and the Tractarians disputed his right to do so and triumphed.

Then some one tried to prove something heretical in the sermon of Dr. Garbett, but the Vice-Chancellor could not see it. Next Mr. Ward, of Balliol, claimed to hold all sorts of Romish doctrines as consistent with subscription, and Mr. Keble defended him. After that Dr. Pusey's case caused much excitement It seemed as if every one wanted just then to unchurch every one else, till Hampden himself, appointed to the See of Hereford, came in for his share of *odium theologicum*, though many of that day believed that jealousy, disappointed ambition, and despair of preferment if Hampden and his followers should block the way, had as much to do with the furious onslaught upon

Hampden as zeal for orthodoxy or dread of lax opinions.

As to Dr. Pusey, the charge was that in a certain sermon he had taught the real corporeal presence of Christ in the elements after consecration. He was suspended for two years. At the end of that time Dr. Pusey meekly mounted the pulpit, and went on where he had left off in some such words as these: "When Almighty God, for secret faults which He knew in me, allowed me to be deprived of my office as preacher, I was endeavouring to explain," &c. He then went on with his subject as if there had been only the casual interruption of a few minutes, and preached a sermon of an hour and a half, in which those who watched for anything not good and orthodox were disappointed.

This reminds me of the old doctor at Salamanca, who, after five years in the Inquisition, was discharged, and also allowed to resume his chair, and while all were expecting a tale of his wrongs, he gently raised his hand, and looking round earnestly, began: "My friends, as I remarked when we last met here," and so continued as if there had been no five years' interruption, but five minutes.

Some of the Tractarian party called Cranmer and Ridley no better than Dissenters. The tendency to ignore the Reformation stirred up the opposition, and the result in Oxford was that, to show that the memory of the martyrs to the Reformation was still cherished in the University, £5,000 was subscribed, and the cross and monument opposite St. John's erected.

My recollections would be faulty indeed if I omitted all mention of Mr. Randall, now about eighty years of age. Randall was a link between the town and the gown, still to be seen surrounded by old Oxonians at the Oxford and Cambridge matches, and at one time never absent from the boat race or other occasion of Oxford distinction. He was educated eight years at the New College School of Choristers, and was scholar enough to do verses and essays, as well as impositions, for the incapable and idle. He probably had some poor gownsmen in his pay, for the demand was far greater than Randall could himself supply. He kept a shop in the High Street for hats and hosiery, with bows and arrows and a few other articles usually required at the time. Many of his Oxonian customers had friendly as well as business relations with him, and not a few are the cases I have heard of his giving timely warning to some elder brother or other member of a family to save a youngster from some imprudent step, whereas there were some tradesmen in Oxford of a very different class, who, after too much credit, would introduce their customer to a money lender, with a hint as to the estate or future expectations. The value of Randall's services has at times been great indeed. He was elected Mayor of Oxford in the year 1859. " How well Mr. Randall was fitted for this important office," says Cox, " I was well aware. How admirably he discharged the duties was loudly expressed at a dinner in commemoration of his mayoralty."

At Christ Church impositions were required to be in the handwriting of the offenders. At Trinity no questions were asked. The barber, then Wilmot, used to contract for them. Mere copying Wilmot would do himself, but for scholarship he had men in his pay. Probably men since known to fame and now in affluence were once the drudges of this college barber!—Very likely; as poverty is a stern mistress and wields a sharp goad too.

Tom Briggs' irregularities caused him to receive frequent messages in this form:

" Mr. Briggs will write out the Psalms for the morning he missed chapel;" or "the lecture which he missed with Mr. Short, and have his name copied in the buttery till sent in." Briggs thereupon was so ingenious as to make a very simple arrangement, as he said, for his greater peace of mind. "I tell the Common Room man not to come near me—it makes me nervous to see his red head and groggy face—but to take all these records of my high crimes and misdemeanours straight to old Budd, my scout. Then Budd takes them to Randall, and receives and delivers the impositions at the buttery, and so I know nothing about these pains and penalties, and live in a state of blessed innocence, till Randall's bill comes in at the end of the term."—That the Common Room man should have told all these contrivances to his old masters, the Dean and Tutors, supposed to be thus partially defeated, is by no means unlikely. Rustication rarely is inflicted but from an accumulation of offences, Tom Briggs' dodge with his impositions perhaps among the number.

No wonder Tom was often in scrapes and found himself in a dilemma, with no choice but to do deeds of which his conscience was ashamed. This was true of all his set; though some I believed to be really at heart much better than their actions would imply.

With several of these men, whom I believed fit for better things, I used to talk and advise, especially over a quiet breakfast table. And if any man has any good genial stuff within him, any milk of human kindness surging in his breast; any soft and silken ties, which mothers weave and sisters strengthen, and all the chaste associations of a parent's roof yet further wind around the heart, linking the cradle with the grave—if these are not all severed and burst asunder, the morning is the season when they put forth all their strength. The excitement of the noon-day, and the riot of the night, week after week, may try them hard and seem to part them ; still, in the daily drama of life, sleep timely lets fall the curtain, and all the virtues the profligate would have stifled reviving with the morning sun send a thrill through the breast and instinctively whisper, "It is not too late to be wise."

College debts from time to time form the subject of many letters of indignant parents, answered by long-suffering creditors in the daily papers. Westfield, of Oriel, took " the benefit of the Act "—debts (" unsecured " of course), £1,250 ; assets one silver pencil case, value about three and six-pence! I remember also J. Blank's hunting coat and boots, among other goods and chattels, being sold at old Wise's auction rooms. It was proved that Blank's allowance from his mother, a dame at Eton, was £250 a year. His tailor's bill alone was £300. Such bills often imply a long course of buying to sell, or robbing Peter to pay Paul. Blank was one of those men who go "tic" for everything, and spend their allowance in fees and turnpikes. But both these cases were exceptional. Fools and knaves are found everywhere, and the same men would be ruin to tradesmen and a heartache to their parents, whether at Oxford or any other town in England. They may also, in some cases, be numbered with the many lunatics at large—men who are mad on one point, and that point the use of money. I could, of my own acquaintance alone, name two, who literally should never be trusted without a keeper in any shop.

As to old Wise's auction room, this was a book auction going on in a room in St. Clement's nearly every day in the beginning of term. Little was sold but the books, pictures and clearings of undergraduates after taking their degree. The room was a common lounge, though, as in other places, many were tempted to bid who never came to buy. Old Wise was rather humorous, never missing a chance of reflecting on college piety or theology when he had any bibles or divinity books to sell. The history of his life was a strange one. He was in Paris in the days of Robespierre, and having dealt with the Court he had a narrow escape with his head; but fortunately, Marie Antoinette's incriminating letter found on him was in English, and he could pretend it was from his sister, as his inquisitor knew no English.

But college debts in a milder form are almost invariably a cruel surprise to parents of small income at the time of the degree, and hang like a weight about the neck of the young curate or the student of the law for years after. The majority of undergraduates never had the management of more than a five-pound note in their hands, when all at once a cheque for fifty had to be apportioned between college dues with wine, confectioners, grocers, clothes, and some twenty different items. A little excess in each being multiplied by twenty soon makes a serious deficit. Some ten years since, Mr. Parker, the old Oxford publisher, told me that my calculation still held good when I said that few took their degrees without owing one year's income, whether their allowance was £200 a year in Trinity, or £1,000 for some rich man in Christ Church.

CHAPTER XVII.

WILD OATS AND A SAD CROP.

I HAVE often been consulted by fathers, and asked the question: "How much shall I allow my son at college?" The last case was that of a millionaire with a son leaving Harrow for Cambridge. I replied, "In your case it matters little as to the money, but more for the habits of economy you would wish your son to cultivate. Now, considering that the social influences of our Universities form no small part of their advantages, I should say, after paying all fees, furnishing rooms, and private tutoring, if required, allow your son £300 a year, but if he hunts or keeps a horse, this must be a separate bill for you to pay." If not the son of a rich man I should have advised the same, only with two hundred a year instead of three hundred.

"Then with this allowance you think he ought to keep clear of debt?"

"Yes, with a little common sense on your part to keep him straight."

"How does he want that?"

"I'll wager you wanted keeping straight last Christmas; with all your experience, does not every year's winding-up draw forth the old remark, 'Who would have thought it?'"

My friend looked rather guilty, and said:

"Then what am I to do?"

"I will give you a hint which will keep every collegian fairly straight, unless he is really a bad one, or one of the lunatics aforesaid. When you give him his first quarter's allowance remind him of the care required in making it do for a variety of different expenses, and say, 'Without treating you as a child and asking what you do with your money, I shall ask you at the end of the term and before you begin another, to name every penny (if any) that is then unpaid.' Say this, and start him clear with another quarter's allowance, and it were a useful lesson if you told him to try to economise for the deficiency of the first term. Continue this till the degree, and not much harm is likely to happen, otherwise debts produce debts, and the more they accumulate the less likely such difficulties are to be looked in the face."

In my time the tradesmen were more disposed to book than to take ready money, partly because a running account binds the customer to the same shop, and partly because men will book ten pounds where they would not pay down five. On this principle Archdeacon Paley (the author of the "Evidences of Christianity") said, "I always make my wife and daughters pay ready money. I admit they only buy what they think they want, but ready money checks the imagination." The profit on clothes and all fancy goods is so large that the extra orders of those who book soon pay for bad debts and long credit. A tradesman said to me in my first term, "I give as long credit as any one." This was to get my custom. I said, "I hope not to require it." He replied, "Yes, sir, nearly all think so, just at first."—In those days your name and college was deemed security, but now society in Oxford, as elsewhere, is more mixed, and an old tradesman told me that he was obliged to be cautious as in other towns.

From time to time, when some Oxonian has been bankrupt, there have been remarks in the papers as if University tradesmen were especially guilty of inveigling young men on to their ruin. This was no more true of Oxford than of other towns. It is not in Oxford only that tradesmen have pressed young and inexperienced customers, that they might introduce some money-lender and make them "fly kites." Some have expected

22*

that the dons would take care of the young men, and heavy have been the complaints of fathers who found that their sons had been unchecked by any college authority in a long course of extravagance.

A statute was once proposed to limit credit, but the tradesmen showed that it would be inoperative. Debts bad in law would be good in honour. The prices would be raised for the risk. Add to this, London tradesmen, tailors especially, used to send their travellers to call at the colleges for orders, and if credit was barred in Oxford it would still be given in London. Others wisely argued, college is a preparation for life, parental leading strings are enough ; if any one leaves his son three years without looking into his accounts he deserves to suffer for his folly. For what man of experience does not know that among his older neighbours a large part live at "Agony Point" to the end of their days; the extras, the "'tis buts," and the contingencies of life eating up all margin and reserve which should place them in easy circumstances, so why should they expect prudence and cool calculation in their sons at the very outset of life?

Nowhere was there less excuse for debt, yet, from inexperience chiefly, nowhere was debt more common than at Oxford; inexcusable, I say, because every man knew his income and started with money in hand. When once in debt to your tailor or wine merchant you lost all control; you must take what the tradesmen sent, had no check on the price, and soon learnt that to continue to give orders, or "to feed the duns," was the only way not to be pressed for payment. Alex, crafty in this as in other ways, when dunned would say, "You want money? Well, Belton or Robinson are in funds, send in your bills to them." —rather precocious this, for college days, but Alex was a sharp practitioner. Alex's door was beset with duns sometimes. I have seen an ostler with a stable bill, a man for pigeon-shooting, a shoe-maker, and a harness-maker, all about Alex's staircase nearly at the same time. Once Charlie found a poor fellow from Abingdon waiting about all the morning for payment for bringing Alex's horse to Oxford, left at Abingdon by him at an emergency. Charlie was disgusted and paid the half-crown, and afterwards told Alex he might repay him if he pleased, and that such shirking was a disgrace to the College. Such painful cases are not common; but when once a man is in debt he feels in an awkward dilemma; it becomes merely a question whether he shall be mean to one man or to another. So truly did Dr. Johnson say, "Regard not debt lightly, regard it as a calamity; it makes all virtues difficult and some impossible."

College debts have been the first step to ruin with many a man, because they not only hamper a man in the early struggles of life, but imply a habit which involves him ever after. The "Debtor's Progress," illustrated by a succession of mental pictures, moves as a sad panorama before my eyes, as I trace some few on the "Road to Ruin" during these last fifty years. There is something truly painful in the "Confession of a Ruined Collegian" when told by a threadbare gentleman now grey and broken down near the end of life, especially when I so well remember how the seed was sown for the very thistles and thorns that have strewed his path. Very few live to know how low such men fall, because at a certain stage they drift out of sight. It was lately stated that a charitable man, who entertained a party of the board or sandwich men, found "the poor gentlemen," once of luxurious living and good taste, represented there, as they notoriously are on the hansom cabs. I once saw a man I remembered as a gentleman commoner at Christchurch assisting in a baker's shop, and the late Mr. Ridgway, of Piccadilly, told me that men of the same class had applied to him and sought the employment of the boys who carry out the newspapers. Large numbers are found in the colonies as mere day labourers, and live among the most pitiable of the waifs and strays; all the more pitiable because a college education implies a sure start in life with friends interested in you, till, as too often, these friends have tried everything and are utterly worn out.

Four of my old friends have I seen down in the world and in different stages of their downfall—a comprehensive illustration and emphatic caution in the spirit of Virgil, where he says, "the descent is nicely sloped and made easy"—so true of the entanglements of debt—"but to get out of the mire of despond and to breathe like a free man again, this is a labour and a work indeed!"

John Fuller, one of the so-called "swell mob" of Merton, hunted and drove tandems, and lived at a rate which only did not astonish me because I did not know at the time that the Rev. David Fuller, of Blankton, drove only a shabby phaeton and kept what John called a "hen butler," and with very little plate to clean. The Rev. David had more than once had a sad shock from tradesmen directing artfully — Fuller, Esq., that the application should fall into the father's hands, and found the deeper he looked the heavier the debts, always understated, for every alleged "only five-pound" bill stared him in the face as seven pounds ten. There had been the usual scoldings on the one part, followed by the usual promises of amendment on the other, till the father grew tired of the worry, shut his eyes and let things drift for peace sake, the poor sisters being consequently stinted in all their little treats and indulgences, and sick at heart at hearing that everlasting "I cannot afford it." After college days John hung on hand, having no taste for any profession that was named to him, and his father as little disposed to advance more money for a doubtful return. So John lived at home. I can't say he did nothing; this never is true. Men must do something; if they do no good they must do much evil. Of course, he had the never-failing inquiries and reminders from "those meddling and impertinent" neighbours, who so often wanted to know what and when he intended—in covert meaning—to relieve his poor parents of his encumbrance and do like other people.

In course of time, when there was not even the apology of youth for his folly, the father died, the little patrimony was divided, and John read the will and found his share a bare thousand pounds, "in consequence of college expenses and advances for debts from time to time." So Doctors' Commons contains in many a document a little family history of some spendthrift sons as well as strongheaded and disobedient daughters pairing off without paternal consent, punished by a comment on their misdemeanours and a poor legacy in consequence.

John had three sisters, all single, whom nature had, I suppose, intended as standing roses in the garden of life. I heard that they had had two disappointments between the three, but nothing that came to anything. Their fortunes, though comfortable if they lived together, became very small when parted. This parting often happens among the fondest sisters when the parents no longer live to keep the family together. Bella grew rampagious, while Lizzy grew nervous, and Martha was all for early services, while both the others thought to make more than one Sunday in the week was dull work indeed. And as to money matters, there is a time when the once fond brothers and sisters change to the colder relations of men and women, and hug their money all the more closely from finding that in this world when their estate comes to ciphers they are but ciphers too. People no longer young and interesting soon find that they must pay their way.

The stocks had slipped from under John Fuller; he was now launched, to sink or swim as best he could. He naturally hated the neighbourhood, and voted the people a bad lot, and had little encouragement, when he so expressed himself, from an old lady who had known him from a child, and suggested that no place ever did suit the man with nothing to do, and that Blankton people would meet him everywhere.

John was now about thirty years of age. Till this time he had floated in society on his father's name and respectability. The natural prejudice that exists against a young man doing nothing was increased in John's case by a rumour that all the family had suffered by his debts and extravagance; but, not to put the friendship of Blankton people to the proof, he very soon removed to London. There he hunted up such few as he could find of his old college friends; but alas! how altered did he find them. Busy and engrossed with the cares and the business of life, and some of them family men, John could hardly realize that they were the same men who used to be as brothers at Trinity with all things in common in college rooms—the present everything, the future nothing, and none of those earnest looks and knitted brows which bespeak an anxiety about things to come.

I used to see John in the Park and to hear of him at divans and billiard-rooms, and at the races, until I lost sight of him altogether. Nearly ten years passed away, when I met Belton, who had by this time inherited a fair estate and was living near Fulham, and he asked if I had heard of old Jack, meaning John Fuller, for report said Jack had been seen looking very shabby and seedy, and shirking away as if ashamed to meet his old friends; it was strongly suspected he was almost destitute. "Jack," said Belton, " was a generous fellow at college. I had far more of his wine and supper parties than he ever had of mine, and once, on one vital point of honour, when my character might have suffered from a cruel libel or misconstruction, he stood my friend in a way I never can forget; so if I could find him out I would certainly pay off old scores."

CHAPTER XVIII.

PAST RECOVERY.

ABOVE four more years passed before I again saw Belton; he at once began about old Jack:

"You could not conceive such an object as I found the once prosperous and fashionable John Fuller, positively like a beggar. 'Ragged misery hung upon his bones.' He would have avoided me instinctively, for he was choked with emotion when he spoke, but he had been too long used to make the most of every chance of a trifle to add to his scanty meals to let a man like me pass unnoticed. Of course we had a deal of confab, and while he was talking of his bad luck and his bad usage, I was thinking more than listening, and thinking what to do. At last I had made my plans, and surprised him by saying, 'Well, you must come home and dine with me.' 'Come home?' he said, with a sorrowful look at his tattered clothes. 'Never mind; not quite in this guise,' I said. 'I have my plans for all that. My clothes will fit you. I remember well when I wore your " pink " (hunting-coat). Here is a sovereign for present emergencies. I'll send you a suit complete. We'll metamorphose you in no time. We will try to look like—yes, to talk of old times. But not at my home just yet. You would rather see me alone, so at my club (the Oxford and Cambridge) at seven o'clock.'

"To suggest first a barber and then a bath—taking my suit, not much the worse for wear, out of the box, which I would send to the bath, and putting his own in—was obvious enough—indeed, too obvious, you would have said, had you seen his sad plight; for misery makes men proverbially neglectful of personal cleanliness. When we met, and I had time to scan my friend—*quantum mutatus ab illo!* He looked not forty, but sixty; naturally he was dumbfounded at first, and like a man in a maze; but part of my sovereign had evidently been spent in drink as well as in victuals; so soon as the bottle passed he became excited, and as all the tables were crowded that day, he was even a little too loquacious and loud, till I cautioned him that the men at the next tables were looking round with admonitory glances at us.

"He had long since spent the last shilling of the thousand pounds, and was living on a family subscription of a pound a week, paid weekly. No wonder his clothes had looked queer. He never was measured for any of them; they were some kind of family contribution too. I could see by the way he gulped down his claret—I did not think it prudent to have anything stronger—that love of liquor had a little to do with his misery.

"The burden of his story was that the world had not used him well—Such men never admit that they have not used the world very well, living to consume its substance and do nothing in return, a system which would make one half-part of the world paupers and the other part relieving officers—He said he had done his best to find employment. Friends had more than once prevailed on City men to give him an interview and hearing, always a very short one. The chief clerk of Catcher & Co. actually told him that his moustache and cut-away coat did not look like business. In short, the clerk took his measure at first sight, and saved his principals the trouble.

"Next, John tried to order on commission everybody's wine and everybody's coals, but 'people were so ill-natured they would not lend him so much as their names'—a mere form, he thought—'for security.' Once he lived with an aunt, but she objected to his smoking and late hours; she was so fidgety, and thought his example did her husband no good, and so they parted, though he could have got on with the said not very steady husband, who apparently liked a boon companion of the looser sort.

"As John soon grew shabby and looked seedy, he found his friends had short memories as to their promises, and were short-sighted when he met them in the streets. He said, 'You little thought ever to see me in so horrid a plight; but the last few years have wrought quite a revolution in my thoughts and feelings and ideas of things in general. Often as I have heard my father warn me that I should one day "come to my senses," I never knew what it meant while I had any one to keep me, but now my eyes are opened. I have awakened as if from a dream, and feel like a creature of another sphere, for this world has changed with me altogether. Even the very streets are quite different, for ever since my clothes became seedy, and clean linen so scarce that I have been forced to button up even in the dog-days, I have found myself instinctively keeping to all the lanes and alleys. I always cut Regent Street and go through Golden Square, not that any one is ever likely to come up to me. No, I walk the town as much alone as if I were dropped from a balloon in some town in Kamtschatka.

"'Various things,' he continued, 'strike me as queer and anomalous in this winter of my fortune. It was easier far, while I could hold my head up, to be invited to all the luxuries of the season than it now is to beg a loaf of bread. The same people who would spend a pound to be genteel will not spend a penny on you to be generous. Very strange, isn't it? There seems to be nothing between turtle soup and starvation. As to friends, the oldest friends and the nearest relatives keep furthest off, for fear they should be asked for anything.

"'Time hangs heavy on a poor fellow's hands when down in the world like me. All the usual lounges and places to kill time fail you. It is wonderful how soon the shopmen descry that you are only looking about and have not a penny to spend. Home, I have none; only a poor garret. I can see daylight through the roof, and you are not expected to be there in the day time. At coffee stalls I eat my breakfasts, and as to dinners —well, I am ashamed to tell you. In fine, warm weather I feel my privations less. Little did I know what a godsend is mere sunshine to the poor: but the winter is awful. I dread next winter. Last Christmas day, old recollections of kind greetings and happy days flooded on my mind, and almost broke my heart. Even the parks can now hardly be said to be open to me. I only dare go there in the early mornings. There are policemen, I have found, in plain clothes, and they eye me and question me. One said he could not make me out—neither tradesman nor gentleman. Perhaps he thought I was a likely man to shoot at the Queen, or do some other desperate deed. As to going near Rotten Row, I should dread the very thought of it. There are glances I might encounter which would pierce me to the soul; and I have not been very near the Serpentine for weeks. The last time, as I was lost in melancholy thought, and gazing at the water, one of the Humane Society's men dodged me and looked so suspicious, I really believe he thought I was going to drown myself. So all I can do is to mope about under the trees, passing gaunt and wretched-looking creatures like myself—men, whose threadbare coats speak of West-end tailors and of better days. Some of these men look at you quite sympathetically—a look quite familiar, as if poverty were a kind of natural introduction, and as if we all belonged to the same sorry and stranded fraternity.'

"I asked John if he had tried to do anything to increase his little income. Every shilling would make a great difference at such a point. He said he had once earned a little when a penny-a-liner—whom he had met while getting a dinner in a boiled-beef shop—was ill, and was paid half earnings for attending at Bow Street; but this did not last. 'This man told me he had eaten and drunk nothing but what he had worked for since he was eighteen years of age; but necessity made him marvellously inventive and sharpened his eye-teeth; and if I had been brought up as he had, no doubt I should by this time have developed some marketable qualities. The worst is, a man rarely tries to earn anything by odd jobs till he is shabby and seedy, and then, on the principle "oft the apparel doth proclaim the man," you hardly get a fair hearing. No man knows the value of money till he tries to earn some, or perhaps to borrow some, for that is just as bad. You remember Alex—always a sharp practitioner with a bet, and a great screw. He owed me, when at Oxford, ten pounds for odds on the Derby.'

"'And won't he pay, in your sad condition?'

"'Pay! No, he cuts me dead.'

"During all this tale of woe, all the more painful because in all such cases nothing more than

BROKEN HEALTH AND—HEART! 51

temporary can be done for a man," said Belton, I could not but notice a certain dry cough of an ominous character. Drink had begun John's downfall; to this resource poverty and loneliness soon lead a man, as if to drown his misery in liquor, while low diet adds a craving for that stimulus; and as the more a man drinks the less he can afford to eat, the lowest depths of wretchedness are reached with rapid strides. So," said Belton, "as I was not afraid of having anything like a long life-annuitant on my hands, I made John an allowance, much indeed to him and little to me."

Two years after I met Belton again, and of course I inquired after John. "Gone! gone!" he said; "last winter killed him. I received a letter in pencil from his bed to visit him in his poor lodging in Westminster. There I found him with a rheumatic attack of a serious kind; the cold and draughts of London streets had pierced the joints of nature's harness; inflammation of the heart followed, and poor John Fuller, but for me, would have been carried in a parish shell to a pauper's grave."

All this came of Oxford debts and extravagance, which swallowed up all that should have given Fuller a fair start, and made the University what it ought to be, merely the stepping-stones to the business of life. So true is the saying that a man without a penny may make a fortune, but the man who begins in debt will rarely rise.

Men go often to Cambridge, but more rarely to Oxford, as a spec, to make a fortune. A senior wrangler they say has achieved a position valued at ten thousand pounds. But save with extraordinary talent and love of study this is a perilous venture, and few parents are able to judge a son's capability of competing with anything so high as a University standard. The head boy of one school has there to compete with the head boys of many; therefore if one sanguine parent is to be gratified, many must lament their own miscalculation and the risk they have run. University honours are as the prizes of a lottery, and the price of a ticket is rarely less than a thousand pounds in money for College expenses, besides three years in time lost to some lucrative calling.

Many parents forget, to their cost, that Oxford is simply a place for education—that is, to train the mind and form the manners, and to make the man. If for these personal advantages a parent can afford to pay, and if it is all he wants, he should not be disappointed; but to ride Pegasus for the stakes to be won, or to woo the Muses, like other ladies, only for their fortune, is a sorry speculation. John

Fuller's father was in no position to venture on his son even the necessary expenses of Oxford, and since, like too many others, he kept no check on expenses, this sad tale of ruin must stand as a warning to others.

CHAPTER XIX.

TRUE TO THE DEATH.

I NEVER entered much into such society as poor John Fuller kept, and which helped his downfall, still I did meet at his rooms in the Albany once rather a fast set of men—men " who had seen life," and who were so far worth meeting that they exhibited a new variety of the *genus homo* and told amusing stories. Of these the most notable was old Tattersall, of Hyde Park Corner, and as a most interesting chapter of life I may venture to repeat one of his oft-told tales :—

" Henry's soliloquy on the death of Falstaff, 'I could have better spared a better man,' is a sentiment that, once in my life, I could have spoken as my own. I could have spoken it over William Habberfield—the friend of my boyhood; for he helped me over Westminster bounds, saved me many a flogging—and was the trusty servant of my riper years in many a sporting expedition; but, withal, the greatest malefactor in all London!

"This sad conviction stole over me by degrees from a variety of evidence, which I have only to relate that you all may think so too, and may also understand how such a man could still retain my honest sympathies to the last.

"Not very far from where now is Belgrave Square, standing alone among the willow beds and the almost impassable ditches that drained them, stood some sheds and low cottages, marking the site of Habberfield's loathsome trade of boiling down horses and other dead cattle. There was also no small trade done, with the Westminster boys especially, in pigeons, rats, ferrets, terrier dogs, and other live stock, 'to teach the young idea how to shoot.' The young noblemen and other sporting characters about Tattersall's found Will a useful man too.

"No one supposed that the dogs had ever cost much to Will; but the consciences both of schoolboys and those who should have known better were, in all sporting matters, anything but scrupulous in those days. Indeed, one and all were well aware that they were encouraging a man who lived in open defiance of the law, and who was known to be the terror of the officers of justice.

"On one occasion some of those gentlemen, having ventured on Will's premises, walked back to Bow Street a little faster than they came. For Will kept bears for baiting, expressly to accommodate some of the Hyde Park Corner clique who met at Tattersall's; and one day, just as a party were turning out with dogs for the attack, one espied the police officers, evidently sent to spoil their sport.

"'Take care, Will,' said Lord Cotham; 'look innocent if you can, for once in your evil life, or the Beaks will have a case against you, and no mistake.'

"'I am ready for them,' said Will. 'Let them come a little bit nearer, that's all; and you, gentlemen, crowd into this stable as quick as you can; the bears know me, and I should be sorry that you should run any risk.'

"No sooner said than done; and now the two rather long-legged fellows, with the staff of authority in their hands, were evidently coming to visit Mr. William Habberfield, when all of a sudden the cages were opened, and out bounced the bears into the yard, and stood turning and grunting about, not knowing where they were at the first moment. Off went the officers as fast as their legs would carry them, amidst no little laughter. Then Will secured his bruins and told his friends to prepare for their afternoon's sport.

"Here, as on other occasions, Will was not the man to think of consequences. Indeed, it is wonderful how he would literally run the risk of the gallows and make little secret of what he had done.

"One day Will said to me, 'I've got a bargain that will just suit you, Mr. Tatt.'

"'What's that, Will?'

"'A horse; very cheap; only stole him last night; cropped mane and tail; his owner would never know him; I'll answer for it.'

"This seemed, then—I know better now—but idle boasting; when he continued:

"'As I was coming home last night from Turnham Green I saw a horse and gig standing at a door—a doctor's trap I believe it was—and no one there to mind him. So says I, 'Will, you might as well ride as walk, if you ain't foolish.' Then up I got, whips off home, breaks up the trap, sells the harness, and keeps the horse for a bargain for Mr. Tatt.'

"True as this was, it seemed but braggadocio,

for such a crime in those days was certainly a hanging matter.

"However, before very long, there was a rumour that made Will Habberfield appear to less advantage—still it was only suspicion, and sporting men are rarely very nice about the character of those who minister to their pleasures, and we are all slow of believing what we should find very inconvenient if it happened to be true.

"A certain exciseman, commissioned to see to the apparent correctness of Will's return, had been traced nearly as far as Will's big boilers, and never heard of afterwards. The police vowed vengeance at the very first slip that Will should make. All Bow Street declared that Will Habberfield—a man whose name was a terror in the then state of the constabulary—had murdered the exciseman and clapped his body into his boiler. But, as no one could say the man was dead, no charge could be made. Still the story was not forgotten. As usual, it served the police for curses loud and deep and supplied young sparks with jokes, and 'How about that officer, Will?' and 'Who boiled the exciseman?' were cant phrases heard very often by our friend, Will Habberfield.

"It is a dangerous thing for a man to break the law; but, seeing that the law cannot act of itself, it is yet more dangerous to stir up feelings of personal pique and private vengeance in those who are already duty bound to bring the culprit within its lash. And such was the jeopardy in which Habberfield had lived for years, when he was so daring as to enter on a new and profitable, but a most perilous, venture in passing forged bank notes.

"At the time of which I am speaking, paper money by the Bank of England was used to an extent at once mischievous to commerce and a cruel snare and temptation to needy men. Forgery became a trade—notes were so ably executed that on one trial two officials of the Bank of England could not agree as to whether a note produced was a forgery or not. Consequently, notes were struck off by the hundred and sold at so much a dozen to the 'smashers,' of whom William Habberfield soon became one. Success and security soon make men bold, and the veil of disguise becomes thinner and thinner, till the eye of justice can at last see through. So, one unlucky day, Will was in a public-house with some notes in his pocket, when two officers entered and made significantly straight towards him. Will in a moment pulled a roll of notes from his pocket, rushed to the fire, with one hand kept the officers at arm's length, while with the other, regardless of the pain, he held the notes in the flames. His very courage proved his ruin. Had he let go the notes they might have been destroyed, but his convulsive grasp saved a portion from the fire, and on the evidence of his burnt hand and burnt notes he was shortly after at the Old Bailey convicted and condemned to die.

"'Honest' Will knew that we could not spare so old a friend and so trusty an ally. He sent for me the same evening, and reminded me that the Home Secretary himself had, in days gone by, had the boldest of rats and the sharpest of terriers at Will Habberfield's crib, and would doubtless remember that one good turn deserved another.

"There are always noblemen enough about Tattersall's to make interest in any quarter, and I had but to name the thing to find friends by numbers. Still, the best terms we could obtain were the usual ones, viz., that if Will would say who sold him the notes, his life should be spared, and a respite of a fortnight was granted for the discovery —if that term expired without compliance, the execution would take place—in other words, as they were always hanging in these days, Will Habberfield would be turned off with the second week's batch of the law's unhappy victims.

"Accordingly James Grant, who was very fond of the bear baiting, and thought it a pity any man should be hanged for passing a forged one-pound note, set off to Newgate to make Will tell his story, and then to look out for confirmation satisfactory to the Home Office. The same evening, I strolled down to Grant's chambers to hear how he had got on. Much to my disappointment he reported that Will declared he never would peach against anyone, so we must try to make better terms with the government; but whether we did or not, peach he wouldn't to his dying hour.

"This high sense of honour from the walls of Newgate and this downright pluck, only added to our determination that so good a fellow should not be left to die the death of a dog. So I asked Grant what was to be done. 'Why,' said he, 'before I left the gaol I thought I would have a talk with the head turnkey, for he has of course seen a good deal of the gradually undermining influence of the condemned cells. Perriman was the name of the turnkey; and Perriman said, "Oh, don't be afraid, sir; all this is mere brag; Habberfield is fresh and strong, and full of good victuals and grog at present; but, now he is condemned, all that is stopped. I have known a man's hair to turn white in a week—so you may expect to see some change in a day or two."'

"We could only hope for the best next day, having sent J. W——, the brother-in-law of the Home Secretary, to see what he could do. The reply was that all the merchants in London would be crying out if any quarter were given to the passers of forged notes. An example they must have; but give up the man who forged the notes and they would have some mercy on him who passed them. Two days after I went to Will myself, and the very clang of the keys and the sound of the heavy doors in those long, dark and dreary passages made me nervous. I found Will in a yard with about a dozen others, all condemned, and most of them without hope of reprieve. As I drew him away from that piteous group, one man said with a significant look a parting word.

"'Did you hear what that man with the fur cap said?' asked Will.

"'No,' I replied.

"'Mind you never turn nose,' were his words.

(Nose means tell-tale.)

"I said nothing at the moment, but thought that all this looked unpromising, till we were seated alone in the governor's office.

"'Now, Will,' said I, after a few common-place remarks, 'you know what I am come about; I have made the best terms I can; it only remains for you to be advised by your friends and to tell me the name of the man who sold the notes, and my solicitor shall make all satisfactory.'

"Will shook his head and bit his lips, and said nothing. Being pressed further, he said—'Now really master,'—he always called me his master—'this is very good of you and the other gentleman, very good indeed, and I should be sorry to disoblige you in any way after all your trouble; but what can a man do—that is, if he is a man, and deserves the name of a man?'

"'Why, look ye, Will,' I said, 'as to what a man can do—should do, you mean—remember you have got a wife and family to consider. Cross the Herring Pond for awhile, and our interest may soon get you back again; or perhaps you may not go farther than Woolwich, and then you may shortly be happy with your wife and family again.' I saw he winced at this. But he was silent, not sullen, but silent; quite as if he felt for me and my disappointment, and did not like to put his negative in downright words.

"The end of all was I left him, as I said, to think about it. Three days of the fourteen were gone, and in three more days I said I would see him again. This was on a Wednesday; on the following Saturday I saw him, and with the same result. Will was pale, and looked thinner, deeper lines marked his features, and I could even see a twitching in his iron nerves; still, by the same kind of stolid silence he respectfully said, 'don't try me.'

"The effect all this had on me was wonderful, I could not rest by day, nor sleep by night. The damp, disgusting smell, and want of light and air, and all the horrible associations of the place—all that made the visit repulsive to me, all fired me with admiration for the man so bold as to say 'I refuse your terms—honour before life—I'll stay here and die!'

"On the following Monday there was a dinner-party at Grant's. He had asked Cotham and all his set, and said 'We'll make a Habberfield dinner of it, Tatt; and you must come.'

"Well, at dinner, Grant and I, 'The two gaol-birds,' as Cotham called us, told our stories, with all that minute detail the company always expects of Newgate stories; and then Cotham said he had consulted the clerk at Bow street, with whom he had some business, and he desired us to see the solicitor for the prosecution, and to learn from him on what information Habberfield was apprehended; for, in all probability, the forgers of the notes, having trusted Will too far, thought it high time, as usual, to hang him out of the way, knowing that dead men tell no tales.

"On this hint we acted—gained the very information desired—ascertained enough to show that Will was betrayed by the very men he was asked to name; and, armed with that weapon of offence, I proceeded, quite in a sanguine humour, to the cells of Newgate.

"This was on the Wednesday, and on the Saturday following, Will's party (that is the next batch) would go to the gallows.

"I used all my powers of persuasion. I blamed his folly—I entreated—I scolded—I entreated again. He seemed more resolved, rather than less, and I left as I came, utterly astounded and out of heart.

"On leaving the cell I said, 'Friday evening you will see me for the last time, Will. Do pray think it all over, and do not let your absurd idea about peaching make you the dupe and the victim of the men who have been your ruin.'

"I went away with a heavy heart. This man had stood before me all my life as a being for whose humour every one must make way. I called to mind the story of the horse and gig, and did not doubt that there was an instance in which he would rather risk his neck than not have his run ; and more and more the conviction grew upon me that if ever man could steadily look and not quail before the tyrant death, that man was William Habberfield. But death, methought, comes so differently in different forms. I could fancy daring death in one rush upon the battle-field ; but to die by inches—the blood chilled and curdled at the heart in these damp dungeons—to hear St. Sepulchre's clock go ding-dong, one, two, three, four, five, six, seven! through the sleepless watches of the night, and to think that all this slow agony should not make a man confess the name of him who was his ruin ; this, indeed, did seem a degree of constancy that required courage more than human.

"Friday evening came. Imagine me imprisoned in Will's horrid cell—Will seated on one corner of the bedstead and me beside him—the grated bars, an earthen pitcher and a pan, and one rickety three-legged table, all the furniture.

"I sat about an hour, talking and talking, and coming round to the momentous question; but very gradually, because I feared that the one word 'no' would strike me to the heart. But—but—you must hear it—the same silent manner, the same compressed lip, the same dogged posture of the head, most plainly, as before, pronounced that his mind, and so his doom, was fixed. And now the clock struck seven, we had only one farthing candle, that only 'makes darkness visible.' It threw a pallid light on those four narrow walls, witnesses of so many a poor wretch's night of agony.

"The gaoler came to the door and rattled his keys, as if to save his saying, 'Now, sir, our time is up.' I got up, and whispered through the bars to the man—'You will oblige me by not interrupting me for just five minutes, to make one endeavour more.'

"'And hasn't he split yet, sir?' said the man. 'Well, I never! Time is very scarce now. Come, Habberfield, don't be a fool. You know what must be at eight o'clock to-morrow morning; so while I step across the yard, do listen to the gentleman.'

"'Yes, Will,' I said. 'This is the last time—will you tell us who sold you the notes? Think—think—before you answer me.'

"William Habberfield looked thankfully upon me and remained silent for at least three minutes; but his lips were closed. I hardly dared to breathe—but—but I saw no change—no quiver—no sign of yielding; at length, hearing the heavy foot of the gaoler returning along the gallery, I said, 'Now, Will, tell us—' Whereupon he looked up, stretched out his strong left arm—his burnt right hand was wrapped in a cloth—then clutched the back part of his thick and bushy hair, and said, with a giant's energy, 'If all ·these hairs were lives, I would not peach.'

"His doom was sealed. I could do no more. Then I said, as well as my voice would let me: 'Then I must bid you good-bye in this world—but—but—before I go, oblige me—do oblige me Will, by answering one question—I mean about that officer who was missing; you heard what was said—Did you boil down that exciseman?'

"'Why, master,' he said, 'you don't think I'd do such a thing?'

"'Yes, Will—this is a time for nothing but solemn truths—I really think you did boil him. So tell me now the real truth—now didn't you?'

"He sat silent, and so I was obliged to leave him. To the last moment he would not say he did not boil him, and," said Mr. Tattersall, with an emphasis as if life and death hung on the truth of his verdict—"it is my firm belief that Will Habberfield did boil that exciseman!"

The next morning ended the days of this robber, forger, and murderer, no doubt; but yet must we add this—in one sense—true and noble-hearted fellow, who thus showed how it is possible for a man to retain a single virtue amidst a thousand crimes.

CHAPTER XX.

AQUATICS—A TALE OF WOE.

As to the amusements of University life, there was no football playing at either university in my day. Boating and cricket, with pigeon-shooting at Bossom's, near the river, were the principal amusements. The pigeon-shooting I have good cause to remember. One Mr. Marsh, of Christchurch, held his double-barrel so carelessly pointed towards me several times that I was induced to change my position, to the great amusement of his friends, when, after a while, bang went one barrel, missing by only a little the brim of his own hat.

In Boating, the bench of bishops was well represented. When Oxford beat Cambridge in 1829 at Henley, there were two embyro bishops in the boat: Bishops Selwyn and Wordsworth, Bishop of St. Andrew's. The Reverend T. Staniforth, of Christchurch College who rowed stroke in that race, writes that Hamilton, once Bishop of Salisbury, and Pelham, now Bishop of Norwich, were in his crew.

The cricket match between Eton and Harrow was also instituted by two bishops, the two Wordsworths—Wordsworth of St. Andrew's and his brother of Lincoln.

Ryle, Bishop of Liverpool, shared with me the honour of instituting in 1836 the annual matches between Oxford and Cambridge.

The first of these matches was played in the month of June; in the same month was the first of the annual boat-races on the Thames. The course was from Westminster Bridge to Putney. The Oxford boat was steered by my old friend, the Rev. J. Davies, of Bath, who lately wrote "The Life of John Russell." Lord Sherbrooke rowed stroke of University College boat. Colonel Peard, Garibaldi's friend, who weighed fourteen stone at nineteen years of age, was a great help to the Exeter boat, which then claimed (doubtful) to have bumped Christchurch, and to be entitled to the honour of being the head of the river. H. B. Mayne, of Christchurch, was as good almost in the boat and in the cricket-field as he has since been at whist. In cricket we had no better all-round player.

At this time we rowed in tub boats. There were no outriggers for some years. We used to think our boats very light, the planks being only about the thickness of a half-crown. As to the style of rowing, it was an egregious mistake. The man who went back furthest and only recovered himself by a toe-strap, was reckoned of the best form. Stephen Davis, who took care of the boats, a big strong man, trained all the crews in this style. No style could be more exhausting or less effective. Stephen Davis had one of the only two boat-houses on the river. Hall, on the further side of Folly Bridge, had also a dressing-room and let out boats, but no college had a boat-house, as now is the custom.

I remember a strange instance of aquatic inexperience in Iffley lock. The Jesus boat got fast and was sinking, from its bow being under a beam in the lock gate. All the crew went to the other end. Of course, the boat was a wreck; it opened flat like a red herring. Every plank was broken or strained.

Lane, of Queen's, a distinguished Etonian, said Stephen Davis was a humbug; his style was absurd; he could not row himself, much less teach it. So Lane was bold enough to train his own crew without any of the go-back form, but with a quick and lively stroke fairly well forward, the oar coming out as soon as straight with the rowlock. With this crew he bumped everything. Once he bumped two boats in the same race, and ended by being at the head of the river.

I remember a supper in Lane's honour, and shall never forget the speech which he made. He gave all the credit to the style of rowing, and said for the future the go-back style, good for nothing but to produce a strange entanglement in a man's interior, must be held to be the absurdity which it was. No one could attribute their success to mere strength of muscle, as they had by no means a heavy crew; "and as to training," he said, looking round, "why, there are three gentlemen here present who are anything but pure examples of morals or of sobriety either."

A book not long since was published to prove, by the testimony of many who had been chosen for the University Race, that there was no kind of danger in such violent exercise. Any one who knows the extreme exhaustion, far beyond that from any other contest, to which men are reduced at the end of a hard boat-race, would prefer his own sense and observation to any number of such witnesses, for those were picked men, men supposed to be exceptionally sound and strong. But Lane's crew could tell a different story. Lane knew that my old friend Godfrey was a first-rate oar and very strong; but Godfrey had promised his father that he would not join the college boat, lest it should interfere with his reading. However, an application was made in the name of the crew to the father, and Godfrey was allowed to row for that term, and with grand results, two places (as aforesaid) gained in one race. The morning of the third race Godfrey felt the worse for the exertion. Strong arguments were adduced to persuade him to row again, and at last it was agreed that Dr. Tuckwell should examine him, and decide his fitness. The doctor said, very emphatically, "No." The same disappointment to a crew of Trinity was occasioned by a similar breakdown on the part of my good friend Locke. I could also name three of my own limited circle, who all said they feared they were the worse for life from college boat-racing. The truth is that while a man can sit on his thwarts he can still keep time and row, however feebly, though so exhausted that in a foot race he would drop.

Sailing on the Isis was very dangerous. Boats were to be seen swamped, and only the masts above water, nearly every day in the October term. At last two men, Graham of Trinity and Surtees of Exeter, were drowned just above the "gut." This caused a consultation among the dons. A foul-weather flag was established, and other orders for safety enforced.

A sudden death in a college makes a deep impression. "What! Graham drowned?" said one; "why, he sat next to me at lecture only three hours ago." "Impossible!" said another, "so fine a fellow; surely he could swim? Only at two o'clock to-day he left me at luncheon." The first impression of all of us was one of utter incredulity. We could not realise so awful an event in such a moment of time, and that so fine a spirit could be so easily quenched. Graham used to sail on Southampton Water, and made too little allowance for the sudden gusts and narrow space of the Isis. He always crowded a deal of sail, which he should have known was especially dangerous, seeing that there was a boat swamped almost every day. Leir, of Trinity—Farmer Leir as we used to call him—and Chapman of Magdalen, with Tyler of Trinity—(the Rev. Charles Tyler, rector of Chatwood), who alone of those three is now living—were in one boat, and had started first, and Graham, with Surtees and Fortescue, soon shot by them in another. Graham was in high spirits, and cried out to Leir, "Much you know about sailing, old Farmer." "It's lucky you know something about it," was the reply, "for remember, my boy, you can't swim and I can."

"In five minutes more," said Tyler, "I saw Graham's sails swept flat on the water. The same gust made us for a moment look to ourselves. We rushed past, saw the hull down, and the top of the mast just above water. We looked anxiously; one only of the three was to be seen—Fortescue swimming with difficulty, from his heavy dreadnought jacket. He had tried in vain to save Graham. We ran our boat on shore, jumped out, and were not quite in time to lend him a hand at the bank. He gasped out with horror, 'They are drowned!' He was dreadfully exhausted; another yard would have drowned him."

The solemn gloom which hung over us all, especially remarkable in chapel that evening—we were all present, as at "Surplice prayers" (29th November)—I never can forget.

The sublime and the ridiculous come near together, never more strikingly exemplified than in Graham's old schoolfellow, Frank Phillips' soliloquy:

"Poor Towser! (Graham's nick-name). Well, the many hours we have spent together! I thought we should be together—never could be parted all our lives—*our* lives! no, my life, I must now talk of—no one else. Graham, I, Wilkins and Gunner chummed together three years at Winchester—never were there three better fellows —Graham the best. We made a plum-pudding every Saturday night for Sunday, and we always boiled it—poor old Towser! — in your night-cap."

No boat but a sailing boat, at this time, was likely to be upset, but in 1859 outriggers came into common use, and very dangerous boats they are, but no practical regulations could be devised for safety, though there was a consultation on the subject, and Cox, the coroner, gave evidence that while there had been only fifteen lives lost in thirty years, nine of the fifteen had been lost in the nine years of these crank boats.

In 1843 two notable occurrences happened on the river. One was the death by drowning of two young men while bathing in the Sandford Lasher pool. Dr. Gaisford's son was sinking from cramp and exhaustion in the rough water of the Lasher, and Phillimore, younger son of the celebrated Dr. Phillimore, sank with his friend in a gallant attempt to save him. The Christchurch Cathedral has a monumental tablet, with an inscription by Dr. Gaisford, and you may see from the railway a spiral column of white marble, erected as a warning to others, near where the two friends were drowned.

The other notable event was that at the Henley Regatta, in Oxford against Cambridge, the ever-memorable seven-oar race—which was in this wise:

Oxford and Cambridge had both shown what they could do at Henley, and great hopes were entertained of victory for Oxford. But Fletcher Menzies, the stroke oar of the Oxford boat, had hay fever. The doctor did not positively say he should not row, but in a race with the "Etona" just before he evidently was run too hard and finished weak. Still, the cry was, "Our stroke will be all right for to-morrow, so won't we walk away from the Cambridge!"

"But next day," said Mr. Adams, author of "Wilton of Cuthbert's," "the town of Henley we found in great excitement." Rumours of all kinds were rife. Some said Oxford had drawn off; others that Cambridge refused to row. Some said the stewards had withheld the challenge cup; others that Cambridge were to have a "walk over."

Perplexity and doubt were on every face. The Oxonians, in their dark blues, were almost ready to tear their colours off.

It appeared that Mr. Menzies, who pulled the stroke oar, a place so essential to success, though ill the day before, had walked down to the boat-yard to take his place in the boat, and while waiting for the crew was taken ill—low diet and excitement culminating produced a sudden change; he fainted away, and was carried to the Inn.

Menzies' incapacity being now certain, the Oxonians began to consider what "emergency" they should select who could best take the stroke oar, and where to seat the new man. But then the question was raised, "Would the Cambridge allow any substitute?"

The terms of the regatta were that a list of each crew should be given in to the stewards, and that no one without this formality should be qualified to row.

Still, with the consent of the Cambridge crew, another man could be taken in. The question was, would they consent?

The Cambridge said as far as they were themselves concerned they would not object; but this was a public regatta—a great sporting match; lots of money had been laid; accidents of all kinds entered into betting calculations: for instance, a man might break an oar or a rowlock; a man might be ill half through the race; none of these accidents would prevent backers from winning or losing money. P.P. races—play or pay—were well known. The Oxford were the favourites; why should the friends of Cambridge lose their chance?

The time had arrived for decision. The hour of starting approached, and it became known that the Cambridge had definitely refused to allow a substitute.

"Well," said a friend, "it is no good staying here in a state of disgust, and to see those fellows row over the course, so let us be gone."

But just then some great excitement was apparent—a loud cheer was raised. What boat is that? Why, it is the Oxford jersey! Yes, and seven men only in the boat. Surely they do not mean, all lopsided—a new stroke and seven men to eight, with the rudder all against one side—with such odds, they surely do not mean ever to try to win?"

"They do, though; and who knows? pluck wins," was the cry.

The Oxford crew, attended by a crowd of enthusiastic supporters, the bow oar's place vacant, now paddled down to the starting post. The Cambridge came afterwards, looking very perplexed and annoyed, and not knowing what to do.

The steward's boat being near, the captain said, " Gentlemen,—We protest against rowing this race. There are only seven men in the Oxford boat : there ought to be eight. We ought not to be required to row against an incomplete crew."

" Time," replied one of the stewards, "is nearly up; we should advise you to go down in time for the start, unless you mean to withdraw from the race altogether, for the Oxford boat will start, and if it comes in first we shall certainly award the Oxford crew the cup."

Thereupon the Cambridge turned round, and had a sharp row, rather beyond the pace they would desire, to the place of starting, and had not a long breathing time before the two crews had the signal to be off.

" Go it, Oxford!—That's your sort, dark blue! Glorious! Hurrah! Well done, seven oars!—Oar and oar still together! It's wonderful!—They can't shake you off.—Dark blue goes on ahead! Hurrah! Hurrah!"

Such were the cries that resounded from a hundred voices; and again:

"It's wonderful! Seven oars wins!"—"They hold their way now.—The wind will help them past the corner if they can but round it! The rudder less against them—they'll win!"

Half the course had now been traversed. To this point the boats had been partially sheltered by the opposite bank from a sharpish wind blowing right across the stream. So far the weaker side of the Oxford boat had been helped by the rudder, which, of course, retarded the boat's way, and the Oxonians, by desperate and gallant exertions, could only just keep level with the Cantabs. But now the river was more exposed to the wind, and all in favour of the side with the three oars, for the rudder could now be kept almost straight, with little impeding backwater. The effect was seen in a moment. The dark blues began to steal away slowly but steadily from the light blues. Presently the cry was, "They are clear ahead," and now, "They have taken their water.—Well done! Give them the back water!—Well done, Oxford! Hurrah!"

The race now was won—a mere procession to the end; recovery for Cambridge was impossible.

As to the excitement—as if all Henley were raving mad at once—that greeted the crew as they landed, no words could tell.

For years after old Oxonians tremble as they tell of the feelings and the triumph of that happy hour.

Alderman Randall, before-mentioned and characterized, made a chair of the timbers of the winning boat, and presented it, inscribed with the names of the famous crew, to the University barge, saved, I was happy to hear, from the late fire, which destroyed the barge.

CHAPTER XXI.

CRICKET OF FIFTY YEARS SINCE.

As to cricket fifty years since, the ground on Cowley Marsh had only recently been made by Mr. Walker, of Magdalen, and was called the Magdalen ground, in distinction from Bullingdon, which for many years had been the only University cricket ground. On Bullingdon, Brasenose College had a ground distinct from that of the Bullingdon Club. Both of these grounds were more for feasting and Tilting (for there was a Tilting club) than for cricket, the Magdalen ground alone deserving notice for real practice and play.

At this time professionals, either at the public schools or at the Universities, were almost unknown. Cowley used to supply some useful bowlers, but all underhand. Such rustics as Hoskings, Blucher and Peter (short for Pieria Bancolari) were well-known names. Very fast and straight underhand bowling, my experience leads me to say, is better to give a beginner correct form and good defence in practice, than round-arm bowling. I have known such players, with very little practice against the round bowling, give their opponents a great deal of trouble.

At this time, Broadbridge and Lillywhite, who were the first round bowlers—as good, if not better than any since—were at their best. "I bowl the best ball of any man in England," said Lillywhite; "and Mr Harenc the next." Mr. Stenning, of Brighton, told me he once saw Broadbridge and Lillywhite bowl sixty-four balls without a run to Pilch and Wenman. Wenman, though of a different style, was almost as good as Pilch; and as to Pilch, Hillyer—the best bowler next to Lillywhite—said he was more afraid of being hit by Pilch, when passed his best, than by George Parr in his prime, and we have no professional now better, if as good, as George Parr.

I think I may say there were about six players in my time at Oxford who would be in the Eleven now. My standard of comparison is this:—The late Vice-Chancellor Giffard scored one hundred and five in one innings at Lord's against Harenc, Sir F. Bathurst, and other bowlers of the M.C.C. when the ground was by no means easy. The Rev.

F. B. Wright and Payne, both Wykehamists, scored sixty each against Broadbridge and Lillywhite in a M.C.C. match, though they had not played against them before. Wordsworth, Popham (the late Francis Popham, of Littlecote), Price, Harenc, Fagg (who played for Kent under the name of Frederics), and Buller were just as likely to have done as much. My own average was double that of Giffard's in my last year, and Daubeney and one other scored as much as Giffard; so I say we had six, though not all in the eleven at the same time, not to be denied now.

This match at Oxford against the M.C.C. with Broadbridge, Lillywhite and Wenman at the wicket, I well remember. Wright (the Rev. F. B.), father of Mr. Wright of the Oxford eleven of 1865, and of Rossal School, and now of Eastbourne, had the same fame as a hard hitter as Mr. Thornton has now, and, if not quite his equal in this respect, better as an all-round player. He went in second innings rather late—thirty being wanted to win—the field set far out for his hitting. Still he hit one for five runs just over the head of little Peter, who was fielding for Mr. Aislabie; he was stepping in and swiping to save the game, as his partner's last bat was worth little. Wright was caught from a dropping ball from that most artful of all bowlers, Broadbridge, and the match was lost by thirteen runs.

I said afterwards, "Peter, if you had been a foot taller you would have caught that ball." "No, I shouldn't, sir," was the reply; "I was fielding for Mr. Aislabie (a Falstaff of twenty-stone), and he couldn't have caught nothing; then why should I? No, sir, I wouldn't catch Mr. Wright out to please the Marylebone gentlemen nor nobody."

At this time the Wykehamists were the best players of the day. They showed the best style of batting, and were particularly famous for fielding. Their rush in to meet the ball, their clean scoop up and quick return, were remarkable. At Winchester they used to qualify by practising till they could throw over a certain building in the neighbourhood, which required a first-rate throw. "The Wykehamists against the rest of the University" was for several years an annual match, and once the Wykehamists played, and won, a match—"The Wykehamists against the two Universities," at Lord's. One Eleven of the school against Eton and Harrow was long mentioned as the finest field ever seen—the same as was said nearly fifty years after of Mr. Game's Oxford Eleven.

The school matches for 1825 were originally

Eton and Harrow. There was much betting in those days. When Winchester at first agreed to play, little was known of them. But when Price was seen bowling down a single stump repeatedly at Lord's the day before the match, the odds altered at once, and men were in a hurry to hedge.

At this time the only schools for cricket were truly schools—the public schools. For there, a good style of play became traditional, and few could learn it elsewhere. There were few professionals, save at Lord's, to teach the art, but there Caldecourt was a first-rate teacher. He and old Sparkes were about this time engaged at Cambridge, so the Oxford ground knew few but public schoolmen—a limited number of course. Nets for practice were unknown; gloves and pads were only made to order and under special directions. I used to wear a pad on one ankle, and a few padded finger-stalls on one hand; one or two only of my friends had some such inventions of their own. So we could not guard our wickets, as now, against twisting balls with our legs—we were obliged to keep them out of the way. When in 1836 I saw Wenman wicket-keeping with a common leather glove on one hand it seemed strange, though Wenman's hands had not the work of players now. He rarely kept wicket in two matches the same week. When Lord Frederic Beauclerc first saw leggings he never imagined they would be allowed in a match —" so unfair to the bowler." This want of leggings necessitated the " draw " between legs and wicket, a very useful hit still, and only unsafe because men know not how to make it. This also will account no little for the long scores of the present day, not to forget there were no bounds, all hits were run out.

And, lastly, instead of, as at present, a place in the Eleven defying all reading for the summer term, we had seven men either classmen or prizemen in the Eleven of 1836—the first of the annual matches against Cambridge. The following men, all known to fame, were in the Eleven in my time :—Vice-Chancellor Giffard, Bishops Ryle and Wordsworth; Dr. Lee, Provost of Winchester; Canon Rawlinson and Charles Duke Yonge, Professor of History at Belfast, a well-known author.

It was a little later that professional assistance became common, though earlier in 1830 I remember Sparkes with the Lansdowne and Bayley with the Kingscote clubs. A man as eminent as Fuller Pilch, though not of the M.C.C., would have a series of engagements to keep him in full practice in county matches, such as Hampshire, Kent, Sussex and Surrey, for these were the strongest counties, but not many professionals had regular practice; few of the county players had constant practice, or rather to be called paid men than professionals. The counties were reduced to select men, who played more on their reputation than on their assured efficiency on any given day. The batting of the professionals was not likely to be strong, because, as Cobbett said to me, "We have no practice but in bowling; our batting must come of itself, except with Pilch and one or two others." This disadvantage, and not inferiority of play, will also account for the smaller scores of those days.

At this time (1832-6) little, if any, but the (then) new round-arm bowling was to be seen in the best matches, and not much of the old remained at Oxford, though Mr. Kirwan, with a kind of undetected jerk as fast as Freeman, if not faster, defied almost all comers at Cambridge; Brown, of Brighton, faster still than Kirwan, was playing at that time, his bruised hip and side after every match proving plainly, as he told my friend Cooke, that the umpires should have pronounced his bowling a jerk.

Whoever looks over the old score books will see "wides" scored from even the best bowlers. As to amateur bowlers, the wides were common indeed in the early days of round bowling. The rule then required an arm nearly horizontal, and this was an action clearly contrary to the nature of the muscles. A little higher you had full command. Caldecourt said that with this little elevation of the hand, "if Lillywhite were not watched, as by country umpires, who thought what Lilly did must be right, he bowled a hundred times better than any man ever did bowl; it was cruel to see how he would rattle about either the knuckles or stumps." So with this cramped style of low bowling little accuracy could be expected but from a man who bowled almost daily, as for his livelihood. This rule of low delivery, however, was so frequently broken that the rule was altered about twenty years since, and a high hand was allowed, and now, so natural is the action, any man can learn to bowl straight. Wides are hardly expected, and wides never were expected and did not score in the days of the old underhand bowling till the ever memorable single-wicket match, when, Osbaldeston being ill, Lambert alone played and beat Lord F. Beauclerc and Hammond. For then Lambert bowled wides right and left to his lordship, and made him lose his temper, and then got his wicket. Then a wide was first made to forfeit one. Now-a-days men speak of underhand bowling as "slows." Much of the old bowling might be so called, but Osbaldeston, Brown, Harvey Fellows, Kirwan, and above all, Marcon, were faster than any round bowler I have ever seen.

To refer to Marcon, for swift underhand bowling, Henry Grace related to me that in one match he saw a young farmer come in with his bat over his shoulder, saying, "Fast as he is, I'll have a crack at him." The first ball that came took his bat clean out of his hand and right through the wicket! So, the old delivery in reality admitted of the greater speed. Still, most of the old bowlers were slow. Budd, Beldham, Lord F. Beauclerc, and Lambert are the names most frequently seen in the old scores, and they were about the pace of Clarke. Clarke spoke of Lambert as a better bowler than himself, as also, he said, was Warsop, of Nottingham. Clarke, aged forty-eight, came forward about 1850, having long lain fallow, as superseded by Lillywhite and his school: and let those who think such a style, at least when brought to perfection, would in these days be hit out of the field, reflect that Pilch, Felix, G. Parr, Mynn, Caffin, and Joe Guy had all tried stepping in and free hitting, and were all obliged to treat Clarke's bowling with great care and respect. The Gentlemen had small chance against the Players in Clarke's day.

At Oxford we used to play an annual match with the town, including the Cowley ground bowlers. Once, when good bowling was unsuccessful, they put in Tailor Humphreys to bowl twisting sneaks, and the wickets fell faster than before Hoskings, one of the best of fast bowlers at that time. The old fast bowling required a very straight bat. In 1848-9, when I captained the North of Devon against the South and the Teignbridge club, men worth a hundred an innings in good country matches, we played the old fast bowling against the round, and in two matches we ripped them up for about twenty-five in each innings—four innings for a hundred runs! But our bowling was really good. My friend Cawston once took three middle stumps in one over! Of course this kind of bowling requires a very accurate pitch. Mr. Budd, one of the slows, like Clarke, I have seen pitch as true as possible almost every ball through a long innings. Clarke had naturally, from a crooked arm, once fractured, almost too much break on his balls, and he therefore always chose at Lord's the pavilion end for his balls to break against the hill. With the slope in his favour his break became too great.

With slows a deal of spin for break and for an abrupt rise was necessary. Budd once bowled me out by a ball that rose over my shoulder and still fell on the wicket. Slows are still tried in good matches, sometimes very successfully, as with Humphrey, for Sussex, but save Clarke and Budd, who from the first practised nothing else, I have never seen any as accurate as they should be. Clarke for four years was never beaten off, and strange to say he succeeded, though too old to field his own bowling well. This is indispensable for a slow bowler, "as also is it," said Clarke, "to be able to send in unexpectedly a good fast ball, to defend yourself when men take liberties with you." In my own play I have always thought I had an advantage in being well drilled with underhand bowling first. It necessitates a perfectly straight bat. Few men play quite straight—men remark it at once when a man does play quite straight—a good proof that such play is rather the exception than the rule.

Canon Rawlinson, then at Trinity College, was one of our eleven—a fair long-stop and a most heartbreaking bat. He would block by the hour: his runs must come of themselves. His play reminded me of a man who asked Pilch, "Shall I be out (a vulgar error) if I don't move my bat?" "No, sir, but you'll be out if you do." Many a shooter have I seen bowled which found Rawlinson's bat still unmoved in the block-hole. Still, by the course of time and the mere chances of the game, he was credited, in an M.C.C. match, with twenty-five runs against Bayley and Cobbett, two of the best bowlers of the day. I was once in a match with him, "The Wykehamists against the University," and when I had scored thirty he had scored five; but since if he had the first ball of an over he usually had all the four; he had three times as many balls as I had and ought to have scored not five, but about a hundred. Charles Wordsworth, of Christchurch, before-named as good at everything, was a brilliant bat—a very free hitter. No University eleven, before or since, could ever have left him out, though in one eleven in Mr. Mitchell's time, every man was known to be capable of fifty runs in a first-rate match. On the Magdalen ground we used to practise with six wickets along the upper side, facing, at a distance of about fifty yards, six along the lower side. Here we had twelve men batting, and twelve men between the rows bowling—no small number for hours daily in danger's way: I wonder they could escape serious blows. Men used to be very careless, but I never saw any accident of much consequence, though a great many narrow escapes. A ball, hit fifty yards, once touched my hair.

As to accidents, I asked old Beldham, who played from the end of the last century, and also Caldecourt, who saw more play than any man from the time Beldham left off, and neither had ever seen any serious accident—none, at least, by which a man sustained material and lasting injury. The most painful I ever saw was that of a son of Sir George Burrowes, who between the innings of a match at Lord's, was struck on the face from a very fast ball from a catapult which was being tried. Burrowes was about the place where a long-stop would have stood, and the ball bounded up from hard ground. Still, though the doctor feared the sight was gone, two years after he said that he was not much the worse. I can also speak favourably from my own long experience; so accidents must have been very few.

Summers, a good player in the Nottingham eleven, died four days after a blow on the head while batting at Lord's—but he did enough, by a journey to Nottingham, to render fatal any case of concussion. Many a man has been hit much harder than poor Summers, for he had no external mark of injury, though the shock broke a little vessel. This I heard from Alfred Shaw, who kindly watched over him from first to last, but could not persuade him to lie by and obey the doctor.

I never heard of any other fatal case among men who played well enough to take care of themselves. But as to "all buts," they are numerous indeed. I have cut a ball for four runs, just shaving the grey head of an elderly gentleman at point—too elderly to be entitled to stand there; and, when I have been one of the twelve practising at Oxford in two opposing rows at the same time, I have often warned men, and warned them in vain, to look out for my hard left-handed hits.

The worst accidents I have known have been from collision. Mr. Slade, an eminent dentist, had to take the benefit of his own art to replace teeth knocked out while running with another to catch a ball at Lord's. Mynn and Box once came into collision: both were too much hurt to play the Kent and England match of the year—the only match in twenty years played without Mynn. When two men run to catch the same ball, the captain should shout, " Stop Smith, Jones has it ; " but this is never thought of. R. Price, a celebrated Wykehamist, before-mentioned, I saw caught on the chin from the point of the awkwardly-extended bat of his partner while crossing in a run between wickets ; his head was forced back so violently he fell senseless, and he said a little more would have killed him. I knew also of a fatal case in a parish match, the batsman hit on the head by a long throw-in : I wonder more accidents do not occur in this way especially. The late Mr. Blackman, in a Sussex match, was hit hard by a quick pelt into the wicket-keeper. He only rubbed his head, and directly went on playing; "too giddy to play," he said, and was soon out : but as good as ever for the rest of the match! There are few blows so hard which some heads cannot stand, and few blows on the head so slight as not in some cases to kill, say the doctors.

As to the choice of the University eleven, there was as much emulation in being chosen for this honour in my time as there is now; of course there always was, and always will be, a certain clique to prefer their own friends, where the claims of those outside the ring are not too apparent. Few had much chance who were not from Eton, Harrow, or Winchester. There was no Marlborough or Cheltenham college in those days, nor for seven years after. Even Shrewsbury was little known for cricket, and when challenging Eton, Shrewsbury is said to have had the reply: "Harrow we know, and Winchester we know, but who are ye?" The Marylebone match at Oxford, and a return at Lord's, were the only great matches. Remember, there were no railways. This made play between rival clubs very difficult. Posting and hotel expenses for young men still "drawing on the governor" were such that we had to consider the purse as well as the play in choosing an eleven. Generally some elderly gentleman gave a seat in his carriage to the young ones, and billeted them about on their friends. Among these, the Rev. J. Prower, of Purton, was very hospitable to our Lansdowne eleven.

We did not carry long carpet bags, with gloves and pads, in those days, though our young players may regard it as quite a primeval cricket institution, and as that "to which the memory of man goeth not contrary."

Now it is pertinent to the present question to chronicle the fact that it was not the speed of bowling, but the fly-about uncertainty of it, that gave rise to padding. Mr. Budd's cricket dress, representing the fashion of his day, was nankeen knee-breeches and silk stockings, a second pair of stockings being doubled down to form a neat roll, to guard the ankle bone. We never saw him wear a glove of any kind, though we have seen him opposed to Mr. Kirwan's bowling. He had also played through the days, not only of Browne of Brighton, and W. Osbaldeston—faster than Jackson's—of whom it may be said that they were not encountered very often; but Howard bowled commonly in Mr. Budd's day, and Mr. Brande bowled very frequently too, and both of these players bowled at a rattling pace, and yet they were ordinarily encountered without pads of any kind.

During our Oxford career, from 1833-36, Price (a name long remembered at Winchester), and a noted Cowley man, old Hoskings, were players who certainly could vindicate underhand bowling from the modern term of "slows," yet there were not half-a-dozen pads of any kind to be seen in the tent. The first greave was claimed as an original and knowing invention, by Henry Daubeney *(fuit!)*, remembered by not a few at the present day, one of the freest of the Wykehamists—then the best hitters and best fieldsmen of all the public schools. By this device Daubeney used to stand up to leg balls far more boldly than he otherwise could have done, and as to the power with which he hit them, he hit Mr. Lowth for a fair seven, near Stonehenge, on ground that in no way favoured the hit.

At that time (1836) Price was the last remaining representative of the old school of bowling, and from that time pads began to grow in size, shape, and variety ; not, we say, because we feared the pace, but simply because no one knew where to look out for what was called round-bowling, but which always was as high or higher than the shoulder.

On the Cowley or Magdalen ground we had no pavilion, only a long tent for dinner, under the victualling of a very remarkable man—a man who might have made a fortune at Oxford with common prudence, so popular was he and so well did he understand University men—" old King Cole." Few men will ever forget Cole's portly figure, his watch chain and seals plumbing a perpendicular clear of his toes, standing before the tent. His fat was disease; about thirty at this time; he died before forty. Cole, though not an educated man like Mr. Randall before mentioned, had, like him, one great characteristic of a gentleman, which consisted in making himself quite at ease with his customers and his customers with him. Cole had decidedly sporting proclivities: he was always ready to make a bet either on a cricket match or on the Derby; and not a few men short of cash found Cole ready to lend. He afterwards kept the "Toy," at Hampton Court, failed and died soon after. No wonder Cole failed, though he was accused of giving only fifty pounds in cash and thirty pounds in wine for a hundred pound bill. His solicitor told me that was quite liberal for Cole, for he had been doing bills for himself on worse terms still!

Naturally Cole was in his own opinion an important personage in the University: he seemed to think it could hardly go on without him. It was "our eleven" and "our gentlemen" always. He would organize the coach for a race at Henley or for one to take the eleven to Marylebone, and was to be seen with betting-book and pencil—common in those days—under the Pavilion at Lords. When Oxford played Cambridge in the first match in 1829, Cole met a similar character and an equally important supporter on the Cambridge side—boasting in the most confident manner of his "gentlemen." "Well," said Cole, "you seem to make so certain, but I'd take odds that two of our bats make more in one innings than all your eleven put together." "Done for £10 to £1." Cole won his bet—he was the sharper of the two. If one side scored more than the other, such a bet would frequently be won, for two bats often make more runs than the other nine. Pooley, with the English eleven in New Zealand, enacted the part of the old soldier in a similar way; he betted that he would write against all the names of the twenty-two the scores they would severally make, and that in six cases he would be exactly right. He wrote 0, 0, 0 all the way down; of course there were six "duck's eggs" in this weak side.

I remember Mr. Ward saying, on the occasion of one of the Marylebone matches, "See the progress of Oxford cricket. I used to play eleven of Marylebone against twenty-two of Bullingdon, and now the club must ask the boys for the odds of two professional bowlers on our side." From about this time the best bowlers used to be more hit about at Oxford and Cambridge than by the best elevens all the season after. So much depends on daily practice and on knowing the exact time of your own ground.

In Mr. Mitchell's day at Oxford, the same side that scored four hundred at Oxford were down for less than eighty at Lord's. Grundy, at Oxford, on that day could do nothing; he said so true and easy was the ground a machine might be made to swing a bat and score there.

The clergy, as University men, were always strongly represented at cricket. Canon Rowsell, and the Rev. A. D. Wagner, at Eton and Cambridge, and also three of our Bishops, were all distinguished. Mr. Justice Bailey, of the Court of Bombay, made the longest public school score, one hundred-and-fifty in an innings.

Lyttelton, Garnier, Wright, and Grimstone were names, both of fathers and sons, in Oxford and Cambridge elevens. The late Rev. J. Ward, of Cambridge, was the son of the celebrated Mr. Ward, who scored 265, which was for many years the longest score, but it was against Norfolk, a weak side, with Budd given. Budd said Ward was missed an easy catch before he had made thirty.

Cricket at Oxford in my day, 1832-6, was more of a sport and less of a business than it now is. We had no cricket elevens from London to play us, and no Oxford and Cambridge match to select and prepare for—the matches in 1827 and 1829 being played before these annual matches. The latter was a very expensive match. The tent and table were open to all comers from Cambridge, and Cole's bill was a disagreeable surprise, above £400! Even contests of one college against another were rare; the reason was that players were not so numerous. Christchurch used to play the University, but rarely did any other college challenge a rival.

The railway system made quite a revolution in cricket. To bring two elevens together was too difficult and expensive in the days of coaches and posting. Knowing this difficulty I was surprised to find a score (given in my "Cricket Field") of Sheffield against Nottingham, in 1772. How well established must the game have been in the northern counties before such a distance could be covered by an eleven in these days. Still the best cricket till about 1840 was confined to the southern counties. The Marylebone played no less than twenty-two of Nottingham about 1820. In the West of England, from Bath westward, there was not a club but the Clifton of any note till 1824, when the Sidmouth played Teignbridge, just founded, as was the Lansdowne the year after; there was a Stalbridge club in Dorsetshire about the same time, but these were all in the West of England. Scotland and Ireland had hardly seen cricket.

CHAPTER XXII.

BOWLING, PAST AND PRESENT—REMINISCENCES.

A FEW words of Cricket in days gone by.

Man and boy, I have played and watched the game for fifty years. I have, as much as any one alive, the right to be called the founder of the "Lansdowne," the principal Cricket Club in the West of England. I can also claim a share of the honour of having inaugurated the annual Oxford and Cambridge Match at Lord's, in 1836. This year, the Jubilee year!

As to the Lansdowne Club, being a small boy at school in Grosvenor-place, Bath, in 1824, I joined in a fund for bats and balls, played every half-holiday on Charmbury Down above Swanswick; and afterwards, being joined by gentlemen in the neighbourhood, we shifted our ground to Lansdowne, about half-a-mile beyond Beckford's Tower, and took the name of the far-famed Lansdowne Club.

At that time, save the Clifton Club and the

Teignbridge Club, near Torquay; and one at Sidmouth, in South Devon; and, about the same date, the club of our old antagonists, with Mr. Floyer, M.P., at Stalbridge, in Dorsetshire—there was no cricket club in the West of England. The wide extension of cricket we owe to the railway system. The expense of time as well as money, when an eleven posted thirty or forty miles, and most of them juveniles and drawing on the long-suffering father's purse—this was a serious difficulty in the way of matches: although, at the same time, the difficulty and the rarity made the contest of rival clubs one of far wider and more momentous interest.

At that time there were a few noted Marylebone players, one of whom was generally hunted up by our weaker opponents, men who when they appeared on the ground were eyed with intense curiosity, and rarely failed to prove themselves very Tritons among the minnows. Among these Marylebone men who thus came starring in the provinces, I particularly remember Mr. E. H. Budd, a player who for the first twenty years of this century bore, next to Lord Frederic Beauclerc, the highest character in the annals of the game as a first-rate slow bowler and a brilliant hitter; he was perhaps the most effective help that any county eleven could invite. But we were not without our lesser constellations too; for Mr. Budd observed to me that our two celebrated Wykehamists, R. Price and F. B. Wright, father of Mr. Wright of Rossal School and of the Lancaster County Eleven, were the two best men he ever met out of London.

Two other All England men, Thomas Assheton Smith, who encountered us at Stalbridge, and whose biography is well known by the pen of Sir Eardley Wilmot, and Mr. Henry Kingscote, who played with the Kingscote Club in Gloucestershire, also were names to conjure by, and men who did no little to raise our provincial standard of the powers of the game.

I have many pleasant recollections of our Lansdowne games, not to mention one very far from pleasant when, at Purton near Swindon, and quite in Mr. Budd's country too, our hospitable friend Mr. Prower, with his customary supper, poisoned four of our eleven, though luckily we had the game in hand, with an unlucky crab which seemed to have combined *cholera morbus* and tartar emetic all in one. Nor must I omit to mention that one of our matches was won by a trick of Charlie Golightly (*quis nescit* old Charlie in those genial latitudes?)

who popped out the best Purton man, Mr. Pratt, *immani corpore*, as he started to run before the ball was bowled.

Now why is it that there is always such a row made when this point of the game, actually specified in the laws of cricket, causes the loss of a wicket? Yet so it is. I remember twice quite a hoot being raised at Lord's, and once when Lord Frederic thought it necessary to speak out and remonstrate and defend the practice, when a too eager runner was thus put out. However, at Purton this popping down the wicket seemed the sharp practice of an artful dodger, as Charlie always was; and not only did Mr. Pratt use strong language at the time, but, said Charlie, "when we met long after at the All England match at Bath, he became quite excited at the recollection, and pitched into me for the old offence, full twenty years after date!"

While speaking of our old friend Charlie Golightly, whom hundreds of cricketers in the West of England will ever remember with esteem and affection, I must include in my half century of recollections the last Lansdowne match I ever played, positively the last; for then the springing of a sinew warned me that there was a time for all things, and Nature plainly cried, "Enough!"

A four-horse break, fitted up to carry all our party from Bath to Kingscote, about the twentieth match our club had played at that pleasant and hospitable resort, was invited to stop at Charlie's cottage and take a parting glass all round.

When he appeared at his garden-gate, bottles and glasses in hand, I said:

"I will wager, my old friend, you have been talking this morning of a splendid catch, on the cricket-ground to which we now are bound, you made full thirty years ago."

"True, indeed," he replied; "and let me assure you there is more in that story than perhaps you have ever heard. Mr. Henry Kingscote, in our first innings, had been hitting a 'square leg,' for four or five runs at a hit, till he scored sixty-five. The match lasted two days and between the two days' play I had a dream that I sallied out from under a certain shady elm-tree and surprised the hitter with a catch. I took the hint from my dream, and made a very long catch near that very tree, just as my dream had foretold."

Well, on we drove to Kingscote, and as John Marshall and I, the only old ones, were talking over some matches of days gone by, forgetting the stealthy flight of time, I observed that in such a match we missed our friend Charlie Golightly, because his first-born was due to make his *début* that very morning.

"Allow me to introduce the baby," said Marshall, pointing to a fine young fellow, one of our eleven, while the others, of course, touched their wideawakes to him and congratulated him on the happy event.

I made some runs in that match; thirty-nine and not out was not a bad finale, but, like all old ones, I was surprised at the many balls I missed which used to be certainties. Many balls, too, passed near my wicket, though I knew where they were, and thought less of it than the adversary, who kept on saying, "What a shave! what a fluke!" At last I stopped this nonsense as follows:

"I'll tell you what, gentlemen: I am here to guard three stumps, and not five, so I claim to play accordingly."

In 1876 I wrote that it would be a great omission if the Lansdowne Club did not celebrate its jubilee last year, as I had the pleasure of attending at the jubilee of their friends of Teignbridge two years before. For while a canon of Norwich, a worthy attorney-at-law, and a late secretary to the Indian Government live to represent our said school foundation, and while I could have been supported by the Messrs. Sainsbury, Mr. Gomonde, Mr. Stothert, and Dr. Falconer, all of Bath, who had seen the earliest days on Lansdowne, the remove to the river-side, Bath, and now its present field beyond the Victoria Park at Weston, the celebration of the fiftieth year of so distinguished a club would not have been without its interest. The hint was taken, and we had a pleasant dinner.

If I have some pride in dwelling on a founder's achievement at Bath, I may be allowed to have no less pride in what I before alluded to, having done as much as any one in instituting the annual "'Varsity" match at Lord's in 1836.

The year 1836 saw the first of the series of the cricket-matches as of the inter-University boat-races, though of both there had been a stray match before. There was a boat-race at Henley in 1829, and a cricket-match the same year at Oxford. There was also a match at Lord's in 1827. The two notables in these matches were Mr. Herbert Jenner, whom, even in the days of Box and Wenman, Mr. Ward deemed the best wicket-keeper he had ever seen; and the present Bishop of St. Andrew's, Charles Wordsworth, who at Harrow, with his brother at Winchester, joined, in 1825, in establishing the School matches for some years annually at Lord's. His lordship was a fine free hitter, and would have been a first-rate player at any day. He played at a time when school professionals were unknown, and at a time that cricket was less a business at Oxford than at present; for now a reading man can hardly hold a place in the Eleven without sacrificing his studies for the term.

Charles Wordsworth was a name long remembered as one of the first scholars of his year, a student and tutor of Christchurch and also a Prizeman; while at tennis, skating, rowing, and cricket he was among the first of his day at Oxford.

I remember a singular bet at Oxford, made and lost from ignorance of the game. A good hitter offered to bet a good under-hand bowler that he did not make him out in a quarter of an hour. The bowler (as runs did not count) put all the men on the off-side, and bowled off tosses, which tried the hitter's cutting powers too severely, and the result was a catch at point.

This was R. Price's tactics. -And who was R. Price? The most distinguished man in the famous Wykehamist Eleven of 1825, who with Knatchbull, F. B. Wright, Meyrick, Christopher Wordsworth, and Papillon were long remembered—just as the Oxford Eleven under Mr. Game is, and long will be remembered—as the finest field ever seen by the oldest player. At the time these men had entered the Universities, Winchester, in point of style, was first, and the rest nowhere.

But the name of Christopher Wordsworth, late Bishop of Lincoln, reminds me that we have had no small number of athletes among the clergy and on the episcopal bench. The Bishop of Lichfield rowed against Oxford in 1829. The Bishop of Norwich was equally distinguished. The Bishop of Lincoln and his brother at St. Andrew's were first-rate cricketers, also Canon Rowsell of St. Paul's, and the Rev. A. D. Wagner, of St. Paul's Brighton, and Canon Ryle with Canon Rawlinson joined me in the first of the annual matches of Oxford *v.* Cambridge at Lord's—a match that Bishop Ryle has the honour of having suggested to me, and arranged through his old Eton schoolfellows then at Cambridge.

At that time we had many men of note, besides Ryle and Rawlinson in later days; Charles D. Yonge, Professor of History at Belfast, then first class man, Dr. Lee, Provost of Winchester, and the late Vice-Chancellor Giffard—all were in the Oxford Eleven.

Giffard the year before scored 105, when Lord's was rough indeed, and against Sir Frederick Bathurst and Harenc. Harenc was a famous Harrovian, one of the earliest good round-arm bowlers.

I doubt if more men of mark, not only at Oxford but also in later life, ever played in a University Eleven.

On the Cambridge side, in their first match, were three of the most celebrated cricketers ever known at Lord's: the present Lord Bessborough Charles Taylor, and Broughton, first-rate at middle wicket or cover point, at which he played *(viret vigetque)* thirty years! The Cantabs played without their King's men, of whom was Kirwan, the swiftest under-hand (either a sling or a jerk) of his day. In the then state of Lord's we could not have stood against him. Though Oxford won the match, little was proved as to the superiority of our Eleven. Lord's in those days, in a hot summer, was clay baked to the hardness of brick—as different from any other ground as a metal billiard-table is quicker than a wooden one ; only those used to Lord's, either in this match or in any other for some years, ever did justice to their play. At this present date, after fifty years, five of the Oxford Eleven survive and not more, if as many, of the Cantabs.

So far did this hardness and roughness combined affect the bowling that I have known a ball from Mr. Mynn rise over both batsman and wicket-keeper into the long-stop's hands ; and I have seen Beagley, so celebrated as a long-stop, with a man to back him up; nor can I forget Caldecourt, when ordered to play on an emergency, saying that he would as soon stand up for a fight, for the blows he expected.

All this is altered now that the Marylebone Club have the ground in their own hands; but in our first University match in 1836, things were at their worst. Charles, son of Lord Frederic Beauclerc, in that match hit square leg above the windows of the public-house, higher up than the mark of a famous hit by Mr. Budd.

And now that I am speaking of fifty years since, the rising generation would like to know a little of the play of those days. There were some good players, but comparatively few among the gentlemen. We had no school professionals, and at Oxford, only one club—that on Cowley Marsh. There was a Brazenose Club and a Bullingdon Club, as old as this century on Bullingdon; but cricket there was secondary to the dinners, and the men were chiefly of an expensive class.

At that time gloves and pads were quite unknown as articles of commerce, though I had contrived a pad for one ankle and three padded finger-stalls which once saved my fingers from a literal smash. The usual style at Lord's, as seen with Mr. Budd and others, was nankeen knee-breeches and two pairs of stockings, the upper pair rolled down to form a pad for the ankle-bone.

No doubt my friends will say there was no such swift bowling in those days, before the round-arm style was introduced. Let me assure them that the swiftest ever known have been under-hand bowlers. Mr. Marcon, an Etonian, was the fastest of all. Brown of Brighton also, and Osbaldeston, Mr. Kirwan, and Mr. Harvey Fellows were all too fast to be safe on any but smooth ground. This bowling was less erratic and easier to keep clear of than the higher style, but in point of pace nothing comes near it. I have known Mr. Kirwan hit a bail thirty yards, and stumps not simply levelled, but smashed, were not of very rare occurrence with Mr. Marcon.

Of course men suffered sometimes. Mr. Budd played for 50*l.* a single-wicket match with Mr. Brand, a fast bowler, and being many runs ahead in the second innings he knocked his own wicket down to give time to finish his adversary that day, for fear that, from bruises received, he should be too stiff to play on the morrow. It was deemed a bold thing that old Lillywhite played the said Brown a single-wicket match, and stood up unpadded through a long innings against his terrific bowling. But the far-famed Beldham did the same thing at the age of fifty-four.

Brown's first appearance at Lord's was about 1820. "Osbaldeston," said Mr. Ward, "had boasted a little too loudly that he could beat any man in England at single-wicket; and only because his pace was so great that few men could hit him before bounds, though he bowled the match away in byes at double wicket. There were thirty byes in a B match. So I let my friends know that there was one Brown at

Brighton who, if cricket was to be made a matter of force and rough play, could beat Osbaldeston at his own game. This resulted in Osbaldeston's challenge and defeat, which he bore with no good humour; for his hangers-on, who came usually to crow at Osbaldeston's victory, turned about and found their amusement in chaffing him on his overthrow. He was so angry that he went to the Pavilion and scratched his name off the list of members. Some time after Mr. Budd asked as a favour that Osbaldeston might be reëlected; but Lord Frederic and Mr. Ward decided the insult was too great, and he must take the consequences of his own hasty act.

Soon after that, a match was made to try Brown in a regular game. Fennex, one of Beldham's day, used to relate how he was at the usual place of cricket resort, the Green Man in Oxford-Street, when Brown, hearing Beldham's name, told him he should soon shiver his stumps next day. " You will let me have this bit of wood, won't you ? " said Beldham, fingering his bat. " Certainly." " Then Mr. Brown we shall see to-morrow." And, indeed," said Fennex, " people did see a sight indeed. Beldham cut and slipped Brown's balls away till he was almost afraid to bowl near him. Once Beldham hit round, for his quickness was wonderful, and helped the ball on the way it was going down to the rails, amidst enthusiastic shouts on all sides." His score was seventy-two; and this, remember, was made without gloves or pads at the age of fifty-four.

I have mentioned three names once known to fame: Fennex, Beldham, and Budd—veterans all. Fennex died above eighty, Budd at eighty-nine, and Beldham at ninety-eight! Three men to whom, as the historian of cricket, I owe more than a passing notice.

Fennex began to play about 1780, and was an All England man for years. It was his boast that he taught Fuller Pilch to bat. Fennex was brought to my notice as nominally the gardener— though fulfilling rather a sinecure office—of my old friend, the Rev. John Mitford of Benhall, in Suffolk, some time editor of the *Gentleman's Magazine*, as also, among other works, the reviser and editor of Pickering's *Aldine Poets*. It was from Fennex that Mr. Mitford gathered numerous cricket recollections, the basis of a series of excellent papers in the magazines of the day. It was from evenings with old Fennex, also, that Mr. Mitford compiled a manuscript which he kindly gave to me in 1836, the nucleus of the *Cricket-Field*, of which, after sixteen years of research and observation, I published the first edition in 1851.

Mr. Mitford related to me his first introduction to William Fennex as follows: "One evening we had been practising so much to our own satisfaction that one of our number, doing what he pleased with the bowling, fancied that for the time, with eye well in, he could keep up his wicket at that moment against Lillywhite himself. Just then it happened that I observed a hale and hearty man of between fifty and sixty years of age, leaning on his stick, with a critical expression of countenance which induced me to say, 'I think from the interest you take in our game that you have been a player in your day.' This led to a few observations about a defect in my friend's play, and eventually Fennex, for he it was, offered to bowl a few balls. Much to our surprise he rattled about our stumps in a way that showed us that in the art of cricket there was, after all, a great deal more 'than was dreamt of in our philosophy.'"

Fennex had a very high underhand delivery, rather after the style of David Harris, as described in "old Nyren," who seemed to force the ball forward from under his arm, pitching with great spin and very near the bat, with a very abrupt rise, and defying forward play. That evening I had much talk with Fennex about the old game and the new. He said, "You can see, sir, my bowling would be queer if I were a younger man; and some of our old bowlers, much as it is the fashion to despise the fair under-hand bowling, would rip up your present players in no time at all. Indeed, people have no notion of what the best of the old under-hand bowlers could do."

This observation was confirmed by Mr. Ward, who said that the round-arm bowling was rendered necessary rather because the old under-hand bowlers were used up, and that there were many difficult bowlers he met in the counties who were not brought forward, and the old style ceased to have its fair chance.

In confirmation of this view of the case, I must cite the case of William Clarke. "Clarke's," said Barker, the Nottingham umpire, "was only the old bowling we had before the days of Lillywhite, only it had lain fallow till the old players who were used to it had passed away, and then it came up new to puzzle all England." Clarke bore witness to the same effect. "Warsop of Nottingham,' said he, "was an excellent bowler in my style, and yet better was the celebrated William Lambert of Surrey, from whom I learnt more than from any man alive."

As to Clarke, although he was too old and heavy to field his own bowling well—and this is indispensable for a slow bowler—I doubt if any bowler of my time ever exercised more influence on a game, nor was Clarke ever " found out "; he never was beaten till the last. You might sometimes score from Clarke rather freely, as you might from any bowler I ever knew. But while quite in his play, it required much patience and no little knowledge of the game to play him. I often hear it said, " Clarke would be nowhere in these days," yet Tinling, Mr. V. Walker, and Mr. Ridley, though very far inferior, on their best days have done no little with slows—and slows too of low delivery—whereas Clarke always maintained that a certain elevation was of the very essence of slow bowling; and Clarke, like Mr. Budd, delivered from his hip. Clarke said, " My success depends not on what is called a good length, but on the exact pitch, the one ' blind spot,' according to the reach and style of the player." He was also always on the wicket with great spin and twist. " Also," said Clarke, " I can vary my pace without betraying the change by my action, and this few fast bowlers can do; and if a man takes liberties with me, I can send it a very fast one as a surprise; or I could not defend myself against a hitter."

As to stepping in, Clarke's elevation was such that you could not judge him till very late; and he could foil you by a twist and a ball pitched a little wide, and then there was a case of stumping made easy.

But with true bowling what do you gain by stepping in? How often is a straight hit from a straight ball stopped for no run, or at most for a single! If you think to lift the ball and hit over the heads of the field, remember that besides the chance of a catch, the segment of a circle your bat describes is so small that, with the least mistake of the pace, and by hitting at all too soon, you are apt to miss the ball altogether, and risk your innings for a very slight advantage.

CHAPTER XXIII.

FELIX, MYNN, COBBETT, AND OTHER VETERANS.

WILLIAM BELDHAM I saw in his cottage near Farnham in 1837, and had some hours of conversation with him. He had lived in days when he and Lambert and one or two others had the game sufficiently in their hands, and when bets were so high as to make selling great matches of no very rare occurrence. He said, however, that there was far less selling than was reputed.

"You may hear," said the old man, "that I sold matches. I will confess I once was sold myself by two men,—one of whom would not bowl, and the other would not bat, his best,—and lost ten pounds. The next match, at Nottingham, I joined in selling, and got my money back. But for this once, I could say I never was bought in my life; and this was not for want of offers from C— and other turfmen, though often I must have been accused. For where it was worth while to buy, no man could keep a character; because to be out without runs or to miss a catch was, by the disappointed betting-men, deemed proof as strong as Holy Writ."

Still it was true that some needy Hampshire rustics would have a visit from some noted betting-men early in the year, who proposed to make things safe for some great event.

All buying and selling was at end when talent was more divided, and no one dreams of unfair play at the present time—though my friend Felix did tell me of one, a Baronet too, who once ventured to make a foul proposal to Alfred Mynn, who replied :

"Get out of my sight, or, Baronet as you are, I am sure I shall be knocking you down."

If Beldham, as I said, could master Brown at fifty-four, it is easy to believe what Fennex said—that Beldham was by far the best of his day, "hitting quick as lightning all round him, the very model of a batsman ; " and it was said that Lord Frederic Beauclerc was formed after him. Beldham's was a green old age. Even when between sixty and seventy he was barred in county matches. When eighty-six years of age he was brought as an interesting relic of the old game into the pavilion at Lord's, much to the gratification of the few old gentlemen who remembered him. The photograph of the old man in his smock-frock is now in the pavilion. About the same time Beldham was welcomed by the gentlemen of the Oval; and when the All-England Eleven in 1852 played fourteen of Godalming at Broadwater Park, Mr. Marshall kindly introduced William Beldham, then eighty-six years of age, who had walked several miles to see the match.

Mr. E. H. Budd confessed to me, "I did so like to make the ring fall back farther and farther as I warmed to my play."

Being a man of great strength and quickness, with fine wrist-play, five feet ten inches in height and twelve stone in weight, no wonder he was a hard hitter, especially in days when bats were heavy. Mr. Budd's bat weighed three pounds, but there were heavier bats than his. Mr. Ward used one that weighed four pounds. When I was at Oxford (1832-6) two pounds ten was a common weight for a bat. Light bats with cane handles were then unknown.

It was from playing against Mr. Budd's bowling that I derived my practical knowledge of what the old bowling was. Mr. Budd bowled, like Clarke, from his hip, with good elevation, and could make the ball rise very high, even when much past his best, above fifty years of age; and his power of spin, which is the characteristic of all first-rate bowling, is what the tired bowler loses at the end of an innings; it is what the used-up professional loses in the course of a school or college engagement; and, above all, it is what old men rarely retain.

Mr. Budd played at Purton, and bowled against Marlborough College in 1852—his fiftieth season, for he began in 1802. He was now sixty-seven years old. He practised the game about four years longer, and died in 1875, aged ninety.

"Lord Frederic Beauclerc"—who bowled in the same style as Mr. Budd—"could not understand how his bowling failed of effect while still so accurate," said Mr. Ward; "but all spin and devil in the ball had departed out of it."

The same was true of William Lillywhite. And here let me observe that few of those who speak of Lillywhite's bowling ever saw him till he was much past his best, and therefore knew not what he once could do. For few players remember him till he came to Lord's, and by that time this famous Sussex bowler was used up. While in Sussex he was famed for an abrupt rise and a quick spin, which in later days no one saw, though on Lord's Ground he was always effective, and up to the last one of the best of his time. Mr. Boudier, one of the best Cambridge players of his day, who played Dean, Wisden, Sherman, Jackson, and their contemporaries, told me that he was more afraid of old Lilly than of any other bowler; his length was so accurate and his command so great, with every variety of pace and elevation.

As to slow bowling, never, but in Budd and Clarke, did I see the accuracy that slows ought to have. A loose ball slow is not to be endured, and a ball with spin on the " blind spot " is never to be despised. And as to the " blind spot," properly so called (for there is just one spot that almost blinds the hitter), both Clarke and Lillywhite knew it was a spot of very small dimension; a fair average length is quite another thing. Clarke thought it was in finding out and hitting this very spot with every player that he enjoyed so great success. And as to Lillywhite, he would pitch up, inch by inch, till he was hit forward, and then he would work away at this critical spot with fast or slow, high or low balls in his own dodging fashion.

And this leads me to speak of what in Lillywhite's early days was called the new game or round-arm bowling.

This invention, the discovery of a round-arm delivery, is usually attributed to a Kent farmer of the name of Willes; but, like the planet Neptune, it might have had two discoverers at the same time. At all events Willes's discovery lay in abeyance until Mr. Knight of Alton gave it prominence. If there was, as believed, a sister of Mr. Willes's who exhibited this peculiar feminine action of the arm in throwing a ball, there were also two sisters of Mr. Knight who also favoured him with throwing instead of bowling, in a barn, in wintry weather; and these ladies suggested the new round-arm delivery which Mr. Knight practised at the same time that Broadbridge and Lillywhite were learning the art at Brighton.

Mr. Knight was one of the chief advocates of the new style, which he had soon learnt to exemplify. All novelties must encounter difficulties in this world; they have to plough their way through the mire of prejudice, and must dare the thorny paths of keen self-interest and jealousy combined.

Budd and Lambert had, a few years before, put the batsmen to shame by a round delivery of a milder form; but Mr. Ward and others carried the old law of hand under elbow against them. And now the principal professionals of the day signed a resolution to play in no matches where "throwing" was allowed; and "thrown out by

Lillywhite" was the ironic style of reporting that bowler's falling wickets in the country papers of the day. The *Sporting Magazine* also, month after month, had letters and discussions on this cricket innovation, and argued very fairly, and indeed prophetically, that with such a system no law defining fair bowling could be carried out; and Mr. Ward, years later, said, "Cricketers are a peaceable set of men, as you may judge by this —I never see bowling about which there might not be a wrangle." Mr. Knight, when asked to define the difference between this new bowling and throwing, replied, "He could not define where the trot of a horse changed into a canter, but men of any eyes could see it." Still eyes see differently; and the experience of years has shown that a line of demarcation was wanting; decisions varied, and the law was conventionally disobeyed. However, the new style, we know, at last prevailed; and the professionals, finding that "they who live to please must please to live," withdrew their protest, with an apology to the Marylebone Club.

It happened rather unfortunately that Lillywhite, as he was the earliest, was apparently the least fair of any bowlers in his delivery. A countryman in Sussex once took my friend to a wall of the ground, and said, "Please to stoop down, sir, till you can only see the top of that little man's hat, and you shall see his hand above it." Very likely, when the umpire did not watch him. Caldecourt said, "Were he not a very short man the high delivery would be so evident that he would never have been allowed to bowl at all." True, Caldecourt did once no-ball Lillywhite, which caused a great outcry in Sussex as a daring heresy indeed; but Caldecourt, as Lillywhite knew, on that occasion was right. For in that match, as one man had been no-balled by Caldecourt, Lillywhite, to show off, as he supposed, the caprice of the umpire, purposely bowled higher than usual. But Caldecourt was too sharp for him, and "dared to cry no ball, even to the Nonpareil himself," as the *Sussex Gazette* indignantly reported.

On this point Caldecourt said to me, "If any umpire will let Lilly bowl as he likes (that is, with his hand a little higher, as at present allowed), he will bowl a hundred times better than man ever did bowl. In different country matches, where the umpire thinks, because it is Lilly, all must be right, it is cruel to see how he rattles among their stumps."

Box said that James Broadbridge was a more

dangerous man than even Lillywhite, for he was an exceedingly artful dodger. So the new system seemed to have been shown forth in perfection by two men at once.

Of course the object of the novelty was to shorten the game, as the batting then beat the bowling. Now as I began to play while the new system was just encroaching on the old, I have a lively recollection that the scores were shortened in this way: the straight balls allowed of few runs, and the wide balls were generally unpunished; for the old cut off the balls (the style of cutting late and forcibly) few players could now introduce; and at the same time a suitable system of leg-hitting had yet to be discovered. To draw between legs and wicket, and to turn at leg-hitting, as if hitting after the ball, which was the old style, caused many misses. But at the present day, or at all events before the high hand was allowed, the round-arm system has lost much of its advantage in shortening the game, because the loose balls do not pass unpunished, and there are not half as many balls which would positively hit the wicket, and consequently the fieldsmen cannot be so accurately placed to save runs.

The first invention in leg-hitting was "the blind swipe," as Lord Frederick Beauclerc termed the hit when you cannot command the pitch; but this is now superseded by various safer hits, and fewer chances are given to long leg; and in the more modern game nothing is more observable than the extent to which players have ceased to score on the on side. Fuller Pilch was at first famed as a free leg-hitter; but he had been caught so often that latterly he gave it up, and I have lived to hear it said Pilch could not hit to leg!

Of course before the round arm there was no little bias bowling. Ashby, a Kent man, was the most remarkable; John Sparkes, who ended his days in charge of the Edinburgh Cricket Ground, was a bowler of the same kind. I remember both as professionals to the Lansdown Club, and was by these old players taught the game. Indeed there was far more bias with the good underhand bowlers than is compatible with round-arm bowling. Old Barker said that all the years he had stood umpire, watching the pitch of the ball, he had seen with round-arm bowlers—save one, two or three—no bias to compare with underhand, though the extended arm gave that appearance. Hillyer and A. Shaw were exceptions no doubt.

As to the command of the ball, the two originators, Broadbridge and Lillywhite, rarely bowled a wide. Until a short time before their day there was no law for wides. Indeed with underhand bowling no such law was ever required; only in a notable match, when, as told in the *Cricket-Field*, Lambert, from the illness of his partner, Osbaldeston, played single-handed and beat Lord Frederic Beauclerc and Hammond, Lambert intentionally bowled "wides" to put his lordship out of temper; and it was only to prevent anything so unfair that wides were made to score. But for years after roundarm bowling was introduced, wides in all but the first matches added no little to the score. I remember a match in Devonshire when one man blocked balls for two hours, and when asked why he did so, he said, "Because I knew my bowlers; only give them time, and I should win the game off byes and wide balls;" which did indeed form the bulk of the score.

The first I remember among the gentlemen who obtained much command over the ball after Mr. Harenc (and he bowled too many wides) were Alfred Mynn, Sir Frederick Bathurst, and Mr. Lowth, a left-handed Wykehamist, who at seventeen years of age was brought up to Lord's to bowl against the players. "Young Lowth puzzled the players so much that the veteran Beagley asked me," said Felix, " ' Can you please to tell me how I am to play that there young gentleman's bowling?' "

In the Gentlemen and Players Match the difficulty has always been to find a bowler. At one time Mr. Harvey Fellows frightened them out; for Pilch played him, said Hillyer, with his head half turned away; and Box said, on such rough ground, no man could play Mr. Fellows. At another time a certain Kentish bowler did the same, both depending on the roughness of Lord's.

But all this time the law of hand under shoulder was in force, and command of the ball was far more difficult. The alteration of that law and the liberty to raise the hand as high as you please have I think, made bad worse, though I must admit it was a necessity. The state of things under the old law was bad because it was conventionally disobeyed; still the law made every young bowler aim at something like horizontal delivery; whereas now, the hand is always higher than even Wilsher's was when John Lillywhite no balled him, dangerously bumping on bad ground.

When the law of hand below shoulder was altered, the argument of those who carried the alteration was this: "No good spinning delivery can result from a high delivery ; let men bowl as they please, and they will find that a high delivery does not answer. The hand therefore will be no higher than it now is, and all dispute about infringing the law will be at an end."

This might be true of the old practised bowlers ; Grundy and Wootton bowled the same as before, and Caffyn knew better than to spoil his shooting and twisting bowling by raising his hand. But with learners the case was different ; they perceived at once that Nature had given very little power to the arm when horizontal, but to bowl with a bent elbow and hand over shoulder was easy enough. So the last trace of bowling in any true sense of the word soon disappeared. In many matches you see a delivery which is vertical right over the crown of the head, though quite fair by law, but in no sense of the word bowling at all, and an abuse which the law never was supposed to intend ; and I am sorry indeed to see in the most interesting matches of the season such a libel on all decent cricket.

The present law has made bowling more common, because easier to learn. A low delivery being against nature is not likely to be a pleasant exercise, while it is particularly discouraging to every beginner.

Fortunately heavy rollers, facilitating the making of true grounds, are more general than they used to be, or much of the present pounding, not to call it bowling, could not be endured. Time was when men were usually put out by good balls, but nowadays the best ball is rarely so difficult as to claim a wicket. Men fall victims often to the mere bumping and the accidents of the game.

Underhand bowling is by no means extinct. It reappears in nearly all long matches. Thus the new game cannot afford to disdain to borrow from the old, though the usual underhand bowling is very inaccurate, and a poor sample of what the old bowling used to be.

Though I regret that this change in bowling was ever made, I see no chance, of course, of going back to underhand bowling with wider wickets. Now that Lord's Ground is levelled with fair turf, and made as easy as before it was difficult, the tediousness of the game is yet more forced on public attention. Three days for a match at cricket when every other contest, yachting included, is confined within the hours of one day, seems absurdly long, especially when twenty-two men are the complement to be kept together.

It has long appeared to me that no game admits

of a more ready adaptation to the powers of the respective sides, and also to the time at their command. Why should all sides, whether with bowlers professional who can hit a narrow wicket, or with amateurs who cannot, always confine themselves to the same narrow mark? If cricket is a diversion and recreation for the serious affairs of life, and not the very business of a life, we must provide for players who can only meet once a week at most, and not for the case of those who can indulge in daily practice. How absurd, then, is it to presume that with any exercise so unnatural as that of round-arm bowling, men, with this occasional practice, can hit a modern wicket! Why should not the stumps at cricket, like the targets at archery, be closer together or wider apart, according to the proficiency of the players? As to the means of effecting this, it were better to have more stumps, or a thick and clumsy stump, than to go on as at present; though the simpler way would be to alter the length of the bail, and to leave to the umpire to say if the ball passed through or not. This would not often happen; and if the umpire, held in check by several in the field, could not be trusted to see this, he could see nothing, so there would be no fear of disputes.

Clubs could challenge each other to play with

bails of so many inches, as agreed. I should like to see a game when almost every ball must touch wood of some kind, either of the bat or of the wicket. No one can be satisfied with the game as it is at present, especially in a dry season with true and hard grounds—with innings of 300 and more runs no match has much interest. Were these scores a rare exception they might mark exceptionally good play; but when they are common what is the conclusion? The thing is too easy. It is like fishing when the fish all seem in a hurry to be caught.

One great reason of the long scores made now is, no doubt, that there are many better batsmen and more defence than there used to be. Now the Gentlemen beat the Players so decidedly in batting that they can afford them any odds in bowling; but for some years the Players beat, not only as now in bowling, but in batting too. The Players used to say that after getting some three wickets their work was done, but now ten out of eleven give them trouble. Still the state of the ground has no little to do with the increased scores, and especially "bounds," from the many spectators, which I never used to see. Only compare the scores of the Gentlemen against the Players at Lord's with their scores at the Oval.

How much longer they used to be! On this point I remember the notable North and South Match at Lord's in 1836, when, with Lillywhite, Cobbett, and Redgate at their best, and with Pilch, Mynn, and Wenman, I think there were eleven men on the ground who could have played any eleven that have ever played since. The scores were about a hundred an innings on that rough ground; but a few weeks later nearly the same men played on the Leicester ground, smooth as the Oval is now, and scored about eight hundred in the match. It was then that A. Mynn made his two famous innings and retired hurt—repeated blows on the leg, received first of all while practising the day before, caused erysipelas, and nearly cost him his life. Redgate said that, bowl what lengths he would, Mynn, by a kind of guess, sent them flying. The ground was shorn of grass, and also quite level and smooth, so the bias would not tell.

On the same kind of ground at Cowley Marsh, Oxford, Mr. Mitchell's eleven scored about four hundred in one innings against the Marylebone Club with Grundy and Wootton, though a week after the same bowlers put them out for about seventy at Lord's. Grundy returned from Oxford quite disgusted, and said to me, "A machine made to swing a bat could play as well as a man on such a ground as that." Not only does hard and smooth ground make the angle of reflection more nearly equal to the angle of incidence in bowling, but when there is no proper turf and the grass is shorn closely away the ball finds no fulcrum to give effect to its spin. It is then that the slow twisting bowler looks out for rain, and a good shower determines the issue of a match.

Then cricketers sometimes depend on the very clouds of heaven, and win or lose by the barometer? Yes; and it is wonderful how much luck has to do with the game, though it still retains its interest. When the Gentlemen claimed, what was then so rare, a victory over the Players in 1846 by one wicket, a chance was given to Guy at point, easy enough had he not just before shifted nearer in. In catches there is nearly always more or less luck. Neither batsman nor fieldsman knows exactly where the ball will fly; add to this that the least roughness in the ground, perhaps torn up by the spikes a minute before, helps the bowler to a wicket; and in the case of a run out the clean fielding that decides it may be assisted or foiled by the state of the ground where the ball is picked up. Lord's Ground is now good, and the fielding all the neater for it.

Another cause of uncertainty is that no man plays quite the same every day. This is true of professionals as well as gentlemen. An old player once said, "Think of the late dinners and the late hours of fashionable young men. How can they play their best when dieted on ice-puddings and sweetbreads, and after being in hot rooms, at parties, till daybreak?" Yes; but the habits of professionals are not much less favourable, especially when country players are tempted to the night-houses of London. Money easily earned—five pounds for a match to a man who hardly earns thirty shillings a week at his daily labour—is easily squandered, and a professional often comes headachy, and half sleepy from beer and tobacco-smoke, on the second day of the match. If a race-horse varies so much that he is faster by fifty yards in a two-mile course one day than another, there is no less uncertainty in the cricketer. I knew a betting-man who used to ask Pilch, who was apt to be bilious, how he felt, before he backed him. A heavy dinner or beer or cigars have disappointed many a man of his innings and spoilt his bowling.

I remember Buttress, one of the best bowlers ever know at Cambridge, whose sobriety was not to be trusted, was employed in a great match, with the understanding that he should be committed to the safe custody of Caffyn, to keep him sober during the three days' play. So the late hours at short-whist, which make some of the Gentlemen's eleven shaky, find a counterpoise in the dissipation of the Players. "They talk over it too much at nights," said Jemmy Dean; "that's what spoils their play." "Add to this," said Felix, "that the jealousy which is the bane of all professions, and turns pale at the success of a rival, is not less rife among professional cricketers. Redgate's reign was a short one. His weakness was known, and there was a general conspiracy to pass the tankard."

Some one will ask, and who was Felix whom we have heard so often mentioned?

His real name was Wanostrocht. Early in life he succeeded to his father's school, well known at Blackheath. But how could a man with a soul for music—he played on six instruments—of a merry, most genial, and social character, and with a genius for cricket withal—how could such a man as this prosper on a small estate in small boys, when all England was tempting him to play in every great match that was on the programme of the year? Felix lived in the day of the famous Kent Eleven, with Pilch, Wenman, A. and W. Mynn, Hillyer, Dorrington and Clifford. "An eleven so good all through," said Martingale, himself among the best, "we did not know whom to put in as last man."

Felix was a left-handed player. I played with him in 1838, the left-handed men of England against the Marylebone Club, with Cobbett, Pilch, and Wenman given. This was the last time the Left-hands attempted an eleven. They had once numbered men strong enough to beat the Right, however small the choice of Left-hands.

Felix was a most brilliant hitter. His cut sent the ball like a shot through the fieldsmen, but the style of it was peculiar. He never shifted his pivot foot (the left to him, remember; the right to another), but always crossed his right foot over. This was also in the style of Wenman, as late of Carpenter, who taught his school-pupils at Marlborough and elsewhere the same style of off-hitting. Saunders also, one of Mr. Ward's time, famed for his brilliant cuts, hit in the same way; and I can recommend this style from my own experience; for then one posture serves for every hit the player makes, as he has one pivot on which to turn, whereas the usual off-play requires a complete shifting of the whole figure. The power of hitting in this form is very much greater ; you have also far more reach and command ; and you can command a ball, however little it rises, and though almost wide, to the off-side, but I think it is peculiarly suited to tall men.

Felix was one of the most celebrated of our players for about twenty years, from 1834-1857, when he played his last match for Horsham against West Grinstead. After which he was afflicted in a way that must be told in his own truly characteristic terms, written in pencil on a book of scores containing this Horsham match and his last innings (31) now before me :

"Farewell! farewell!
"May 20th, 1857.
"After this match I was most kindly admonished by Almighty God, being struck down by paralysis when in the enjoyment of good health.
"N. FELIX."

Harassed by an action-at-law about some pictures, and working double tides to redeem his loss, poor Felix's o'er-wrought brain suffered paralysis. After a time he could amuse himself with his pencil, and living at Brighton, entertained his many old friends with his recollections of happy days gone by. The kindness and the sympathy of the many friends he had made wherever he appeared in the cricket-field found substantial expression in a collection to buy him an annuity, making him comfortable in his declining days.

His friend, Alfred Mynn (both were for some little time in Clarke's All-England Eleven, for with both pleasure at last spoilt business), had experienced the good fellowship of the community of cricketers in the same substantial way. After his long and expensive illness, brought on, as related, by the accident at Leicester, he was voted a benefit, very well supported, at Lord's.

Felix was so great a favourite, and made so many friends at matches at Manchester, among other places, that some merchants determined that they would retain so genial and musical a companion among them, and offered their interest to secure him an appointment in the Customs worth 1,200*l.* a year. But unluckily the office, though promised him, was one which was not again filled up; otherwise Felix had never known the trouble that laid him low.

Other cases we could name in which the friendships of the cricket as of the hunting-field have set men forward in professional life. Dr. E. M.

Grace, I believe, has found that the sympathy and good-fellowship of old cricket-friends have, every now and then, lent him a help in professional life.

One word of Felix's opinion of William Clarke's bowling. " The first match I played I scored freely from Clarke's bowling, and in my next match I was to meet Clarke at Nottingham, on the side of the All-England Eleven, and found myself saluted on the ground as 'Clarke's master.' But this was a mistake indeed. I never mastered Clarke to the last. In this Nottingham match he took every wicket in his first innings, Pilch's included. Clarke could bowl four distinct kinds of balls. He said, ' If a man is fast-footed he is ready money to me ; as he plays me forward from his ground. I have practised a ball on purpose, and put on a screw that just misses his bat.' "

Of this Nottingham match Clarke once conversed with me and said, " Mr. Felix stepped in and hit me the first ball ; next ball he made a feint as if to do the same ; but thinks I, you don't mean that, I know ; so I sent in a fast over-pitched ball, and, as he was made up for back-play, he was taken by surprise, and knocked his own wicket down."

Felix and Mynn were the great supports of the

Gentlemen's Eleven for years; but as cricket supplanted business, latterly they joined Clarke, who found no slight advantage in having two men of their standing to meet the gentlemen of the different counties. Mynn's playing weight was from seventeen to eighteen stone, but even after he was twenty stone he played in the All-England Eleven, and Parr said he still was worth playing, though double the weight of Caffyn and Wisden at that time. Felix and Mynn were alike in this: their amiability and good-nature were perfect sunshine in the cricket-field; and if, as to moral qualities, I add to them the names of Cobbett and of Wenman, I should name two of the first players of my day, who as Nature's gentlemen have left the most pleasing recollection on all who ever played with them.

Cobbett was one of the few all-round players— first-rate at bat, field, and bowler. Pilch said Wisden was the best all-round man of his day; one of the best judges in the Marylebone Club replied, "I thought you would have said Cobbett." How many other professional all-rounders have we had—really good at all points—Martingale, Dean, Caffyn, Griffiths, Hayward, Grundy, Hillyer, Jackson, H. H. Stephenson, Tarrant, Oscroft.

As to Cobbett, first-class as a field, his batting

was always valuable when runs were scarce and play difficult, but his bowling deserves some remark. Cobbett, like Lillywhite and Broadbridge, began as an underhand bowler, which I suspect is no bad beginning. Certainly every batsman should begin to play underhand bowling first—to learn good defence and straight play. Cobbett's was the most easy and graceful, and by far the fairest of all bowlers. His hand was quite horizontal in the delivery, level perhaps with his elbow, but not the least above it. Then his wrist was thrown back at the last moment, and his fingers being lapped round the ball, the ball left his hand quite with the action of a man spinning a top. When I have blocked a shooter from Cobbett, the ball would continue spinning before my bat. Of course the result of this delivering was that his balls usually shot or rose abruptly in most erratic style, and if aided by the ground were difficult indeed. He did more with catches than with wickets, as compared with Lillywhite, whose glory it was to " dig them out " and root up the stumps, never so pleased as when stumps and bails went flying. I have heard the old man say depreciatingly of bowlers, " O, they may catch 'em out, or stump 'em, or run 'em out; but I like to see 'em clean bowled out."

Cobbett almost always pitched true, but few consider how often great spin and rise of the ball make it miss the wicket. Cobbett was once tried with an undefended wicket, and much to his surprise he only hit the wicket once in six balls; but though true on that occasion, perhaps the ground or the novelty of the attempt was unfavourable to him on this trial.

This trial was made before members of the Moor Park Club at Charliwood. Redgate, when their practice-bowler, was tried in the same way and with similar results. To pitch true to a wicket is one thing, to hit it another. Let me suggest to some of our few bowlers now—those who have good spin and bias, no others—to try the experiment before they draw any inference as to Cobbett and Redgate, very true bowlers both. Of course the bowling must be of fair length, and not be pitched up for the purpose. With the present high bowling and less bias, I think more than one in six must hit the wicket.

This experiment was tried in consequence of an amusing after-dinner match at single wicket. A man, laughing at his friend's bowling, offered to play him on these terms:

"You shall play as usual before the wicket, and I will play behind the wicket;" meaning to place himself where long-stop stands. Of course in that position every ball was a hit, of which he made not a few before the other could hit the undefended wicket.

As to Lillywhite, one day at Cambridge he backed himself to hit a wicket against the catapult, and won. But few nowadays have seen the old catapult. The ball, set on a block of wood, was struck by the recoil of a strong spring. You could set it to any length, and vary the power, but the precision was not exact. It was invented by Felix, and much used to teach his friends and pupils at Blackheath. In 1842 Cobbett died of consumption, the death of Dorrington, Lockyer, and Tarrant among others. For men of that tendency the heats and colds of the cricket-ground are trying. On a fine genial summer's day all is healthful enough; but snow hangs over head and sometimes falls in the month of May (witness Bloomsbury's and Hermit's snowy Derby-day), and fieldsmen are liable to stand shivering on wet grass in any bad season. Add to these causes of danger men continue to play too late in life, when no longer proof against chills and sudden changes.

Two veterans, Jemmy Dean and Pagden, both famed in Sussex, made a single-wicket match, in

1871, when too old and heavy to run. Jemmy was to run his own hits, but Pagden, weighing about eighteen stone, was allowed a deputy; still this could not prevent his exertion as bowler in saving short runs. Jemmy, though carrying a fair rotundity of belly, his watch-chain plumbing a perpendicular as he stood, made above fifty runs, and then knocked his own wicket down.

The amusing part was, that Jemmy had appeared at the wicket with two bats. "What do you want with two bats?" we asked. "Why, because I mean to stay in long enough to wear out one to be sure," was the reply. Pagden was beaten in more senses than one—beaten physically as well as in a cricket sense.

Six months after, as I made inquiries, Dean said, "I am sorry, sir, I played that match; I killed my man. Pagden was never well after it, and is now dead and buried."

Jemmy Dean was a shrewd and amusing fellow, always in a good humour, and, like Ben Griffiths, most popular with the ring, at Lord's and elsewhere. His name will be found in the scores of all the great matches from about 1837 to 1860. Both as long-stop and bowler he was first-rate. His balls rose with a spin very abruptly when the ground favoured him. He was an awkward bat, but did good service frequently, when "Go it, Jemmy!" was the cry from the men of pewter and of pipes. He once said, "Sir, that ball was such a shave that with another coat of paint I should have had your wicket;" and when asked why the manufacturing counties were so strong at cricket he said, "You see, sir, that cricket is a gift; and there is such a blessed lot of them up there to have the gift." One reason for the pre-eminence of Yorkshire, Lancashire, and Nottingham is no doubt that those men can play not only enjoyably but profitably all the summer, and return to the factories in the winter; whereas in the agricultural counties cricket involves a sacrifice of employment, and we frequently see sad cases of used-up professionals. Even Pilch was in difficulties before he died; and not a few find that the usual resource of keeping a Bat and Ball public-house brings more temptations to drink than return for their little investment.

One more word of Jemmy Dean. One day we were discussing the decided superiority of Mr. W. G. Grace over all the players we had ever known. "No doubt, sir," said Dean, "Mr. Grace stands in a class of his own; but as to his many runs you must take into account that there is no break in his practice; early and late in the cricket

season, and perhaps before, Mr. Grace is always
playing. Now with most others there is a break
and interruption; that takes the eye off the ball,
and then the hand and eye do not act together.
I have experienced this in my own case very often.
You remember I used to keep my wicket up for
hours even when I did not score much; and I do
assure you, sir, that by the middle of the season
my eye was so steady *I could see the stitches on the
ball.*" He added judiciously, " It is the calm and
steady eye that does it—the eye that does not wink
but follows the ball right up to the bat. Why,
lots of gentlemen I have bowled to used regularly
to shut their eyes when the ball pitched on the right
spot, like bad shots when they pull the trigger."

Of Mr. Grace I would observe that as to his
batting two points are almost peculiar to him:
first, that in every position he is always seen with
a bat perfectly straight—and playing nominally
straight is another thing. When I heard this
remark of Pilch and Wisden and a few others,
" See how straight they play!" this bore witness
to my remark that playing perfectly straight is a
rare exception. I have seen Mr. Grace again and
again save his wicket from a twisting ball just by
an inch of the shoulder of his bat, when others
not quite straight would certainly have lost a

wicket. The second point is that Mr. Grace never plays wrong. When quite a boy (for he was in the Gentleman's Eleven when seventeen years of age), after exulting in a fine hit, he was not to be tempted next ball in the exuberance of his spirits like other young players. He knew his reach and would never risk a hit beyond it.

To these two points in Mr. Grace's play we must add another—the strength of constitution and the stamina that enable him to do no little of the bowling as well as of the batting in two matches a week all through the season. I remember one of the best of Mr. Mitchell's Oxford Eleven who, after the London week of University matches, in which he fielded as cover-point, an anxious post, was so prostrated by over excitement that he was obliged to lie by for a fortnight.

Others who show fatigue less lose their vital energy, however unconsciously, in different degrees. For this reason the hand and eye of a cricketer, as of a sportsman on the moors, often fail, he knows not why. Mr. Grace must suffer too, more or less. Still the surprising point is that the balance of his energies yet remain enough for innings of three figures, and wickets in proportion.

While speaking of Ben Griffiths, let me record

that he once hit Bennet's slow overhand bowling for four sixes, twenty-four runs in one over. This we never knew equalled, though Mr. Thornton once scored twenty off one over from Mr. Buchanan. And Griffiths among the professionals and Mr. Thornton among the gentlemen are the two hardest hitters of my time; I mean in their usual style of play. Griffiths however, never seemed to exert himself or to play for sensational long hits. With Mr. Thornton, hard hitting used to appear his chief amusement at the wicket; and be it observed, if a man is indifferent to defence and stands prepared for hitting only, most good players would hit hard. Still in Mr. Thornton's hittings there is something remarkable; his eye, and the timing of his hits, must be perfect to produce results so brilliant. When a boy, in the Eton Eleven, I remember that he hit over the pavilion clean out of Lord's; and these straight hits require positive strength. Mr. Thornton also hit one hundred and forty yards square to the leg at Canterbury; but such square hits are less a question of strength. But he also hit, from before the Brighton Pavilion, straight over his bowler's head, one hundred and forty yards, clearing the entrance-gate into the road, measured by me!

Mr. H. Fellows has hit as far as a hundred and thirty yards to long field; and several of that gentleman's hits used to be quoted as *ne plus ultra*. Among little men and light weights, Mr. F. Wright and Charlwood equal anything I remember. Height to a batsman is a great advantage; but if to these two we add the name of Mr. Mackeson we shall see that first-rate players may be of all weights and sizes. Few men play like Hayward and Daft, making the most of their height.

And here I may speak of remarkable feats with bat and ball.

Mr. Cazenove at Oxford bowled down five wickets in one over, a fifth ball being once allowed by a mistake of the umpire.

Redgate bowled out Pilch, Mynn and Stearman in one over, and shaved Pilch's wicket with the first ball.

Hill bowled or caught Messrs. Hornby, Ridley, and the late F. Grace in one over.

Tom Adams got every wicket in both innings of the Zingari at Woolwich in 1849.

Mr. Kirwan bowled the ten M.C.C. wickets at Eton.

Dr. Grace got every wicket at Canterbury with slows in one innings, after his innings of 200 runs.

Mr. V. Walker in Surrey *v.* England in 1859,

got every wicket in the first innings, and scored a hundred and twenty-eight runs in the same match.

Wisden bowled out every one of the South Eleven while playing for the North in 1850.

Clarke bowled Day twenty-seven overs without a run in 1850.

At Lord Winterton's the same side which scored 100 in the one innings made none in the other!

Mr. G. Yonge bowled forty-five balls without a run to five of the All-England Eleven, and got one wicket.

Dean bowled fifty-seven balls against good men without a run.

Grundy has bowled eighty-four and Wilsher a hundred balls for one run.

Lillywhite and Broadbridge bowled sixty-four balls without a run to Pilch and Wenman.

Mr. Marcon bowled four wickets in one over against Swaffham in 1850.

Stephenson bowled out three of the Kent Eleven in three balls in 1858.

Atkinson, for the United *v.* All-England Eleven in 1859, bowled thirty-six balls for three runs, and then bowled fifty-two balls for no run.

In the North *v.* Surrey, in 1857, when Surrey wanted only one run to tie, Jackson got out

Stephenson, Miller, and Griffith in three successive balls, but others remained, and he could not save the match.

Next to Mr. W. G. Grace's innings, so well known, Jupp's carrying his bat out from first to last against Yorkshire, the strongest Eleven in England, in both innings, surpasses all in my recollection. And recently Mr. Scott, for Australia against Yorkshire, made winning hits of three sixes and a four, twenty-two runs, in one over.

There is nothing more remarkable in cricket than the effect of the mind on the play and also on the fortune of the match. I once asked Charles Taylor—I was at the time publishing the *Cricket-Field*, and therefore compared ideas and experience with all who excelled in any particular point of the game—" Can you give me any hints as to the captain's part in the game?" "The greatest point of all," he replied, "is to make all the eleven play their hardest and their best." Yes, there is a certain earnestness, a *vivida vis animi*, which has a marvellous effect on the energies of the field watching out, and a no less depressing influence on each man as he comes in. How often have we seen runs made at the rate of sixty or seventy an hour, when the cry is that only a dozen are wanted for a tie, and it takes half-an-hour to make that dozen, if indeed they are made at all! Again, we have seen maiden overs, or runs made with the greatest difficulty, when all of a sudden there has been a catch missed or an overthrow made, and at once the play seems slack, the charm is broken, and from that moment quick run-getting has been the order of the day.

The effect of mind is also shown where the field support the bowler. Never choose a bad fieldsman for his batting; the loss is felt not only in the balls he may fumble or the catches he may miss, but in the way he may paralyse the bowler and demoralise the whole side: few bowlers can do themselves justice, and no good bowler dares to try experiments when he doubts the support of his field.

The effect of mind is above all exemplified in that panic which sometimes ruins a match. "Once establish a funk," as the players say, "and the men go down like nine-pins." In one Oxford and Cambridge Match, two good men were well set and winning at seven o'clock, when time is usually called. The game seemed so hopeless to the Cantabs that they agreed as it were to go through the form of the thing till half-past seven, and not waste the following day. Two wickets fell in the next five minutes; the rest went in with a bad light and nervous, and the game was lost by three runs. Of the ball that settled the last man, Mr. M. cried out, in his disgust, " Why, I could have played such a ball as that with a broom-stick!"

On account of the said effect of mind, I had rather play with ten earnest men than have an eleventh who smokes or chaffs or even looks indifferent; and I had rather see one match where men play heart and soul to win than ten matches of stale professionals who play as a matter of business, and never start till the ball is hit. County cricket should therefore be encouraged; for, in such matches only, except perhaps the matches of the Schools and of the Universities, are you likely to see good and earnest play.

It is the same mental energy that we miss, and which makes play less worth seeing towards the end of a season. We may have the same men who did much execution with bat or ball in the earlier matches; but as regards their play, their outplay especially, they are not worth by any means as much as before; nor would I go very far to see them. No; we want a superfluity of mental vigour for first-rate play. Charles Taylor always said he could not play "Tophole" a second match the same week. Good play requires, above all things, concentration. The same catch which would be made early in a game at point, or at slip, or short-leg especially, is missed later. Attention flags, and the mind is off the stretch. "And so in long-stop's work," said Mr. Hartopp: "it is the end of an innings after the first hundred runs that tries the correct style of a long-stop; for if he does not work easily to himself as a proficient, it is then that runs come apace." Mr. Hartopp played as long-stop for nine years at Lord's. "Harvey Fellows' long-stop" was the name he was once well known by, from his effectual support to that gentleman's terrific bowling.

Concentration is more, not less, required in batting; and I believe that men are as often out because the mind tires as because the body is fatigued. The great secret is "to watch them well." Stand well up, as Daft does, and as Hayward used to do—and no two professionals played in a better style—and look well at the bowler. Never talk to the wicket-keeper or any one about you. Think only of playing the strict game. It is as necessary to preserve the mind as the body in its proper attitude. Above all, do not think or long for any ball on or off before it comes; if so, you are very likely to make a mistake, and a fatal one—and for this reason: the

30*

muscles act with the will, as in table-turning. You are told to wish the table shall turn to the right or left, and you unconsciously use your muscles in that direction. It is on the same principle that if you go in to bat, thinking many runs are wanted, you rarely play the same game. If you go in against the runs, for last innings, the mind is off its balance. You are not only more nervous but hurried, and play differently. You cease to play by habit; the mind begins to work, and there is a hesitation in your play. So true is this, that, with young players especially, first innings is odds in favour of victory. I have observed that out of the first thirty-nine Public School matches the side that had first innings won twenty-seven, and the side which went in second only won twelve times. In the latter case each man feels the responsibility resting on himself individually, whereas with the other side it is divided with the Eleven in the field.

No doubt there are other reasons for the disadvantage of second innings—one also which I may term mental, namely, the discouragement when a long score is made against you; but we must allow sometimes for worse light and nearly always for worse ground, though the mental influence is paramount. Hence the importance of right habits of play. As you practise, so you will play. A rigid habit of playing the game, and nothing but the game, strictly, when you practise batting, will alone form a counterpoise to these tricks of fancy and betrayals of the mind. It is in vain to say, when hitting wildly, "I should not do this, but play steadily in a game." The muscles will twitch according to the habit that they have formed, and produce a fatal hesitation, if you do not play positively wrong, at that critical moment when the ball pitches. You find *one law*, or one tendency and inclination *in the mind*, and *another law* or tendency *in the members*, so that you *cannot do what you would*. A great moral principle is thus exemplified in our noble game.

CHAPTER XXIV.

THE OLD KENT ELEVEN.

AMIDST all the recollections of myself and of my cotemporaries, no cricket matches hold a more prominent place than the glorious contests of the old Kent Eleven, and the annual fixtures of "Kent against England," which continued to be the great match of the season for twenty years, from 1834 to 1854; and I think all true cricketers will admit that the achievements of the county of Kent deserve a distinct record for the spirited endeavour of Lord Harris to bring together all the talent of his county, and once more to give Kent its old-time superiority as second to none as a cricketing county—and this year beating both Australia and Yorkshire!

Kent has as fair a title to be regarded as *cunabula Romæ*, the cradle of cricket, as any other county. Hampshire has too often been pronounced to be the earliest county that showed any excellence in our national game;

but Kent may justly claim to share the honour with Hants. Kent was the earliest antagonist of Hants, and the earliest county that played single-handed against All England; and much betting would appear to be customary at this great match, for, as early as the year 1748, the Law Reports contain an account of an action brought in the Court of King's Bench to recover two bets of twenty pounds each—a very large sum in those days—laid on a match of cricket, which had been played by the County of Kent against All England. The question raised was whether cricket was a game, within the meaning of the words of the statute, "or any other game or games whatever," by the 9th of Anne. The court held "that cricket was a game, and a very manly game too, not bad in itself, but only in the ill use made of it by betting more than ten pounds on it; but that was bad and against law."

An exciting match of Kent against England was also, in 1770, made the subject of a mock heroic poem, written by one James Love, comedian. The heart-stirring crisis of the match is thus described:

> "To end th' immortal honours of the day,
> The chiefs of Kent once more their might array:
> No trifling toil e'en yet remains untried,
> Nor mean the numbers on the adverse side.
> With double skill each dangerous ball they shun,

> Strike with observing eye, with caution run.
> At length they know the wished-for number near,
> Yet wildly pant and almost know they fear:
> The two last champions even now are in,
> And but three notches now remain to win,
> When, almost ready to recant its boast,
> Ambitious Kent within an ace had lost.
> The mounting ball, again obliquely driven,
> Cuts the pure ether, soaring up to heaven.
> Wallock was ready—Wallock, all must own,
> As sure a swain to catch as e'er was known;
> But whether Jove and all-compelling Fate
> In their high will resolved that Kent should beat,
> Or the lamented youth too much relied
> On sure success and Fortune often tried,
> The erring ball, amazing to be told,
> Slipp'd through his outstretch'd hand, and mock'd his hold
> And now the sons of Kent complete the game,
> And firmly fix their everlasting fame."

Kent held its high position as a fair rival for All England, without men given, till the year 1879, by which time, by the formation of the Marylebone Club, Middlesex had become powerful as also had the counties of Surrey and Sussex; so Kent was obliged to be reconciled to no higher honour than that of competing in ordinary county matches.

But, in the year 1834, it was observed that in every great match the Marylebone Club drew their foremost men from Kent. So Kent, after measuring its strength with Sussex, the land of Broadbridge and Lillywhite, once more aspired to the honour of playing England single-handed, and thenceforth "Kent against England" formed part of the season's programme for the lovers of cricket.

In this year, 1834, Mynn, Felix, and Wenman, who were the main supports of Kent during the whole of the series of All-England matches, headed the eleven. They were assisted by Mr. Harenc, who was then the first gentleman bowler, second only to Lillywhite, and also by Mr. Herbert Jenner, as fine a wicket-keeper as ever appeared at Lord's.

Alfred Mynn, though not so much to be depended on at that time, with Mills, did the rest of the bowling; but then Pilch always played against Kent, not being then naturalised in Kent, though afterwards he received an annual retainer from the county, and was engaged at Canterbury to instruct the club, and was quite the father of the Eleven. Mr. Fagge, who played often in the name of Frederics, showed by far the best form of batting in my day at Oxford. I remember well when he was practising against pelting for bowling on Cowley Marsh, for the first county match, his college having given him permission to go to Lord's for this great occasion, on which he too played a fine innings. Mr. Knatchbull also played. He was a celebrated

Wykehamist and a dashing field. However, Kent did not win. Cobbett and Lillywhite as bowlers, backed up by Pilch and Marsden, on the side of England—and the said spinning bowlers, be it remembered, powerfully aided by the rough state of Lord's ground—were quite enough then to account for Kent's defeat.

Next year, in 1835, Hillyer and Clifford joined the Kent Eleven, and Kent, though beat in one innings in the first match, returned the compliment in the second by winning in one innings also.

In 1836, Pilch still played against Kent, and the match ended as a drawn game, but much in favour of Kent, and the next two seasons, that is in 1837 and 1838, no Kent and England match was played; for Alfred Mynn's illness would have deprived Kent of his powerful assistance.

In this year the Marylebone Club made a Kent and England match at Town Malling for Pilch's benefit, and Kent won after a most exciting contest by only two runs. Kent also won the return match this year by three wickets. It was in this match that Redgate—than whom no man more frequently took Pilch's wicket—bowled Pilch, Alfred Mynn, and Stearman in one over! and, said an eye-witness, he drank a glass of brandy (I hope not a large one) between each wicket as it fell.

Fuller Pilch, Dorrington and Tom Adams had joined at length the Kent Eleven—good men all. Mr. Haygarth remarks that at this time there was a remarkable number of good bowlers, gentlemen and professionals; never so many at the same time. These comprised Sir Frederic Bathurst, Messrs. Alfred Mynn, Charles Taylor, Harenc, Sayers, Whittaker, Kirwan, and Craven; and as professionals, Lillywhite, James Dean, Hillyer, Cobbett, Redgate, Clarke, James Taylor, Fenner of Cambridge, T. Barker of Nottingham, George Picknell of Sussex, Tom Adams, Hodson, Martingell, Good, and Bayley. One reason there have been so few good bowlers is, sometimes, that the spin and devilry of the bowling is spoilt by overwork; our bowlers play too many matches, with exhausting school engagements before the season opens; and some belong to All England travelling elevens and the like. In this way our bowlers are spoilt and used up. Fine bowling requires a delicacy of hand and free, fresh and lively wrist. This natural movement of the hand is soon replaced by a mechanical jerk of the shoulder, and by a twist and wriggle of the whole body.

In 1840, Kent, at Lord's, lost by 76 runs; but

E. Wenman, their captain, wicket-keeper, and almost their best batsman, was ill, and unable to play.

"This," said Felix, " was uncertain to the last; and then, I am sorry to say, I saw a certain noble lord, and another who should have had a nobler spirit, walk down to the gate at Lord's and obtain the earliest information, and then remark, 'As Wenman is not playing, and that makes all the difference too, we can now afford to back England. We need say nothing about what we know of Kent's loss.' I have lived always a poor man, but I never condescended to such tricks as that."

It was in this match that Tom Adams hit a ball to the top of the tennis-court, and made a hole in the tiles which long remained unrepaired, a visible record of the hit.

In 1841, Kent won the first match by two wickets, though Felix did not play. In this match Wenman stumped three men, and one of them he stumped off Mynn's swift bowling—happy for Kent that Mynn had any wicket-keeper to do him justice. It was in this year first that Martingell joined the Kent side—a fine field, fair bat, and very useful bowler of a medium pace.

In the return match of this year, Felix was

again absent; still Kent beat All England in one innings.

These Kent and England matches continued more frequently in favour of Kent, to 1853, but their last victory was in 1849, though Kent probably would have beaten England in 1851, for in that year one game was drawn decidedly in their favour. After the year 1854 Kent never was matched against England even-handed till 1862. It is evident that the strength of the county depended on some five men—a host in themselves; and with the youth and strength of these men, the glory of Kent and the proud boast of one county standing against All England departed too.

The men to whom I allude were Mr. Alfred Mynn, who played thirty-two out of the thirty-three games which, "out and home," were played from 1834 to 1854. Chiefly owing to Mynn's injury at Leicester, and the long illness which followed, there was no Kent match in 1837 and 1838, nor did Kent record a victory up to that time. They had too many amateurs, and that in a day when gentlemen had no school or college professionals, and did not practise as earnestly as of later years. Messrs. Harenc, whose bowling had declined, Fagge, Knatchbull, and Norman were good men all, but not quite up to the mark of All England men. But in 1839 and 1840, Thomas Adams, Dorrington, Fuller Pilch, and Martingell added a power of strength indeed; and these, with Mr. Walter Mynn, Hillyer, and Wenman, for ten years—from 1839 to 1849—played about even with All England, winning nine matches and losing ten; Martin and Hinkly coming in as useful recruits in 1845 and 1848 respectively.

Mr. Herbert Jenner played the earlier matches; and Bayley, Chief Justice of Bombay, in 1842-4; and Mr. C. de Baker played occasionally during the whole series, from 1841; and Mr. Whittaker for five years.

Pilch and Martingell were not native players, but naturalised only by professional engagements; but other counties had similar advantages. Felix, like Martingell, was Surrey born; but Felix kept his school for years at Blackheath, a denizen of Kent.

To continue my recollections of these Kent and All England matches after 1841. In 1842 the first match was played on the Beverley Ground, Canterbury. Fuller Pilch came out with a grand score of 98, and Felix kept him company for 74, against eight bowlers: Lillywhite, Dean, Barker,

Hawkins, Fenner, Good, Butler, and Sewell. These I may well enumerate, to show how strong was the All England Eleven at that time. The whole score of the first innings was 278; and this was long odds in favour of the side that scored so many in those days, yet England scored only 12 less; and Lillywhite, getting seven wickets, put the Kent Eleven out for only 44 in the second innings, and All England won by ten wickets. In this match Guy made 80 for All England; and with one forward drive, for which he was famous, he made seven runs, without any overthrow.

In 1845, old Lillywhite, though fifty-three years of age, scored 30 and 7. The byes—14 and 15 lost by England, and 10 and 12 by Kent—seem in these days too many for good fielding, but we must remember the fast bowling and the state of the ground before heavy rollers were known. But on any ground, for byes and leg-byes, five per cent on the whole score used to be reckoned fair fielding.

In 1846, at Lord's, the match was a very exciting one: England won by one wicket. Lillywhite, then fifty-four years of age, bowled beautifully, and got ten wickets, though Martingell, Dean, and Clarke took the other end, always the Pavilion end; for old Lilly always said, "I shall have the lower wicket, and after that you can have which you please."

This gave him both the slope of the ground and, usually, the summer breeze at his back. But this slope was too much for the great natural twist of Clarke's slows, so Clarke preferred to twist against the hill from the other end.

In the return match at Canterbury, Kent, with an innings of only 94, won in one innings, though Alfred Mynn, their great bowler, was unable to play—the only occasion on which he failed to appear for Kent. In the Gravesend and Essex match, a week before, he and Box had come into painful collision while rushing for the same ball, and both were too much hurt to play in the match.

In 1847, at the match at Canterbury, Felix caught out seven at point, at which place he was an excellent field. Dorrington was almost as good at cover as Hillyer was at short-stop, so the Kent fielding was very strong. When Wenman was absent Dorrington kept wicket. Tom Adams was capital at long-leg, and Martingell good anywhere.

By the year 1848 the best players were growing old. Fuller Pilch was forty-eight, and Wenman and Felix forty-five years of age. Great then was the value of a new colt like Hinkly, who got sixteen wickets in one match, and all in the second innings, though Hillyer and A. Mynn took the other end. Still England won. Age had begun to tell, and England, after the railway system had been so long developed, drew good men together from north and south, east and west, to take away the last chance of Kent any longer standing against England. William Clarke now appeared on England's side. "Against Clarke's bowling all the best players," says Mr. Denison, "*muffed* their play. Pilch scored only 2 and 13, Dorrington 11 and 6, A. Mynn 1 and 4, Wenman 2 and 0, and Hillyer 2 and 6." In the return match, however, the scores were small, and Kent won without any help from Hinkly's bowling.

Mr. Haygarth relates that the match was won by Mynn hitting the ball to Parr, who, instead of throwing it up, ran off and pocketed it as the perquisite of the man who last handled the ball. This caused an alteration in the custom; the ball was henceforth ordered to be given to the umpires, and thus an unseemly scramble for the ball after the game hit was obviated for the future.

In 1849, Kent played without either Wenman

or Dorrington, and Clifford, not so good a performer, was chosen as wicket-keeper. In this match Lillywhite greatly distinguished himself: he was then fifty-seven years of age, yet he clean bowled five in the first innings; Wisden and Clarke bowled at the other end, but neither of them did by any means as much to win the match. Wisden and Clarke, however, being now in full force, usually made England very strong. As to Lillywhite, whoever wishes to judge correctly of his powers must remember that up to this late age no man did more with the ball. Whatever bowlers took the other end, Lillywhite almost always had his share of bowled or caught, and many clean bowled; he almost despised catching men out: he liked to dig them out, and send the stumps and bails flying. What if they had seen him, with all the freshness of his spin and abrupt rise which characterised his bowling, in his earlier days in Sussex!

In 1850, at Canterbury, though Fuller Pilch was fifty, he scored 29 and 51; when Wenman at forty-seven scored 30 and 29 for Kent: but Kent lost by fifteen runs.

In 1851, at Cranbrook in Kent, in consequence of rain, the match was drawn, but decidedly in favour of Kent. This was one of the All-England matches got up by Clarke, and at a time that Daniel Day was second to no bowler of the day, at least under Clarke's guidance. "Be sure, Day, while you bowl for me," said the old one, "that you never let any man go on playing you back. Pitch well up, and drive them on to forward play, and I will set the field to suit you. The worst ball you can bowl is a short-pitched one." "Clarke and Day," said Mr. Haygarth, "bowled 128 balls to Pilch and Wenman without a run." I give this on his good authority; if true, it beats all the feats ever heard of with the ball.

In 1851, Kent had lost for ever Dorrington and Martin; though Wilsher had commenced his career; but by this time Grundy had joined England, which registered a victory by four wickets.

After 1851, A. Mynn's bowling failed, he had grown very heavy (about twenty stone), and in 1853 Kent had the humiliation of following—*Solve senescentem*—their innings. Adams was aged forty, Pilch fifty-three, Wenman forty-eight, A. Mynn forty-seven, and Hillyer forty. The glory of Kent had departed. The extent to which Kent depended on one limited set of famous players may be judged from this—that, out of the thirty-three matches played between Kent and England at Lord's and in the county :

A. Mynn	played	32
Hillyer	,,	32
Adams	,,	25
Wenman	,,	23
Felix	,,	20
Martingell	,,	20
Dorrington	,,	17
W. Mynn	,,	16

These men were all playing together between 1839 and 1849, during which time Kent could hold her own with England, winning, as I said, nine matches to the ten won by England.

Hillyer was indeed a great acquisition. Kent having small choice of bowlers had now found a first-rate man in Hillyer to divide the work with Alfred Mynn. We must distinguish this great bowler as Alfred, because his brother Walter was also a valuable aid to the Kent Eleven. Mr. W. Mynn I heard say that Hillyer bowled in the most difficult style of any man of his day. If Lillywhite was rather more accurate, Hillyer's bowling was very fair, being as much lower than that of most others as Lillywhite's was higher. His delivery had, as a natural result, all the more spin. Spin and abrupt rise and shooters therefore characterised Hillyer's as also Cobbett's bowling;

Hillyer and Cobbett having the lowest and the most easy and graceful delivery of any men in my remembrance. Hillyer's bowling had also this great advantage, that it was faster than the average, while at the same time, which is very rare, the pace did not annihilate the bias of the ball. The ball, after pitching to the leg, would often cut right across the wicket, almost like Mr. Buchanan's; and this twist on a fast ball gives many a catch to the slips.

As to the slip required for Hillyer, the pity was he could not act two parts at the same time, for Hillyer was the best short-slip ever known—a capacity which he had many opportunities of displaying against Mr. A. Mynn's terrific bowling. Indeed it was most fortunate for the Kent Eleven that they had a man to do full justice to Mynn's fast bowling as slip as well as in wicket-keeping. The catches Mynn caused to the slips would have been lost with many other men than Hillyer.

Next to Hillyer, as to the difficulty of his bowling, of no man have I ever heard so much praise as Buttress of Cambridge. "Buttress," said Fred Miller, "could almost make the ball speak. I played him in one match and by him only it was that the United won against the Parr's All England

Eleven. I offered Buttress five pounds if we won; but I had to commit him to the care of Caffyn to ensure his remaining quite sober enough to bowl during the match."

I well remember Buttress's bowling in that match as excellent indeed—the pace was rather slow, but the bias and the dodge very remarkable.

William Hillyer played for Kent from 1835 to 1855. In the last season he fell and broke his thumb, and afterwards ceased to play, but commonly stood umpire in great matches, and died, like not a few professionals, of consumption in 1861. Mynn and Wilsher followed him to the grave.

William Martingell was the youngest of the Kent Eleven, being under twenty years of age when he first joined it. Still Parr played for All England at seventeen, and Mr. W. G. Grace as early; and I think I may add Daft to the list of young All England men. Before William, old Martingell, William's father, had been an old-fashioned bowler, who, like Fennex and some others of the old school, gave such a spin to a fast underhand ball as would grind the fingers against the bat. William Clarke's balls would also punish those who despised "the slows" in the same way, and Clarke used to boast that he sent men back to the pavilion for their gloves to save their fingers.

W. Martingell made himself first known as a Surrey player, but being engaged under Fuller Pilch on the Kent ground he made rapid progress, and, though not quite a first-class bowler, he was useful at the wicket almost in every match he played. His batting and fielding were both good, and he was one of the few good all-rounders. He was chosen by Clarke for his All-England Eleven. Such a player must undoubtedly have been valuable to Kent. Like some others of the professionals of that day, I am happy to name William Martingell as not only popular generally, but as one of the humble friends of not a few of the gentlemen and patrons of the game. After a good engagement with Lord Ducie at Woodchester Park in Gloucestershire, he ended with being a successful tutor to the Etonian Eleven.

Edward Wenman played for Kent twenty years, and had turned fifty-four before he retired. He was a very powerful man, fifteen stone, and six feet in height, and well built. He was by trade a wheelwright and carpenter, at Benenden, in Kent. The Benenden Cricket Club was long celebrated, and supplied not a few players to the County Eleven. At Benenden, Wenman till lately lived, and was greeted with the greatest respect and friendship whenever he made his appearance on a cricket ground.

Wenman was always valuable to his county as a captain and manager of a match, second to none of his day; also, as nearly the best bat; and Dean thought he was equal to Lockyer or to any one he had ever seen as a wicket-keeper. " His left hand was so very good," said Dean ; "and you know, sir, a wicket-keeper gets very few chances if he can only stump with his right."

Wenman's play was not with a long reach forward like Pilch, but more like Parr's style and that of the modern school. Wisden said Wenman's back play was the best he had seen ; and when once I saw him play Redgate's many shooters on Lord's, which then was hard like baked clay and as rough as the road, I thought him the most efficient man in a difficulty I had ever seen ; though to Carpenter I have reason to award equal praise for the same style of play and play under difficulties.

Richard Mills was a great support to the Kent Eleven in its early days. I played with him as one of the Left hands against the Right at Lord's in 1838. He was a fair bat, very hard hitter, like most left-handed men, and one of the best bowlers of his day. He was one of the recruits from the Benenden Club. In 1834, Mills, with only Edward Wenman, played a strange match: those two against an eleven, and they won easily. Mills' bowling, however, was less required when Hillyer joined; and Mills did not play with them after 1840. He was then forty-two years of age. He retired before the more glorious days of Kent.

John Gude Wenman was cousin of Edward Wenman: he was a fine left-handed bat, and capital field at long-slip or cover-point. He only played five matches out of the thirty-three.

Chief Justice Bayley, the same who scored 152 in the school match of Eton against Harrow at Lord's, played three matches with his county. He was worth playing for his batting, but he was better still in the field, either at long-leg or cover-point. So the Kentish field was strong at all points—though most of the men were rather sure and steady than quick, being past the age of great activity. Thirty is the extreme limit of quick fielding. The best fielding ever seen is in the Oxford and Cambridge matches, at least as regards quick fielding. Professionals, from their unintermitting practice, are generally more sure and safe at a catch, but they are too mechanical, and rarely move till the ball is hit, and therefore cannot cover as much ground, and are rarely as good runners in the field as gentlemen ; as to running between wickets, the gentlemen generally beat the players by twenty per cent. at least.

Edward Martin joined the Kent Eleven in 1845, and played with them till 1852, eight seasons. Though not young, being thirty-four years of age when he joined, he was accounted a most excellent field, especially at long-leg, and he was a free hard hitter. He once kept a cricketer's shop at Oxford, and there he secured the friendship of a wealthy collegian, who set him up in a farm at Leominster ; after which Martin's history is one of those remarkable ones which every now and then tend to show that fact may be stranger than fiction.

Martin had kept on his Oxford shop while attempting to attend to his farm on the borders of Wales. Finding the two incompatible, he sold his stock, and with several hundred pounds of the proceeds in his pocket, he one morning left home on a favourite horse. This was in the year 1849, and from that day to 1869—twenty years—nothing more was ever heard of him. But in November of that year a man fell from his horse and was killed, at Barcombe, near Lewes ; and Martin's relatives were astounded by the news that he whom they had long lamented as probably robbed and murdered had lived unknown so many years, and might then be seen a corpse at the Royal Oak Inn of Barcombe. His papers had disclosed the address of his friends.

Edmund Hinkly was also one of the Benenden recruits, a left-handed bowler as well as bat. His bowling for the last five seasons of the Kent and England matches was valuable indeed as a refresher to the failing powers of Kent; for Alfred Mynn was now past his best, and Hillyer wanted more assistance against the powerful bats of England than could be found in Martingell alone, whose bowling was not quite accurate enough for first-rate hitters, and never very difficult; but Hinkly's bowling was ripping indeed. He was rarely opposed to George Parr without getting his wicket. He bowled fast round-arm with much ease to himself—a good delivery with a break from the leg which was very destructive. Once, at Lord's, he took seven of the wickets of England in the first innings, and all in the second, though Hillyer bowled all the time—one of the most remarkable feats in the history of cricket. Hinkly honestly belonged to Kent, though his name will be found sometimes on the side of Surrey, because he once resided near the Oval.

Tom Adams is a name that heads, I think, every score of the Kent Eleven for twenty-five matches. In every match Adams went in first. As a severe and slashing hitter, he had thus the advantage of such loose balls as come before the bowlers have settled down to their work, and also, since free-hitting means guess-hitting, he could more easily guess the rise of the ball before the spikes had cut up the ground and made the spin of a Cobbett or a Redgate more effective still. With the bat he did his full share; his average was from 10 to 12 an innings; but his fielding was first-rate, and he was a very useful change bowler. He bowled on the left, and, consequently, over the wicket—a style that renders "leg before wicket" easy to decide, though of proportionably rare occurrence, but at the same time the light is often obstructed and the player balked by the umpire; though, no doubt, the bowler then loses the advantage of some of his bias and of a spin across the wicket.

CHAPTER XXV.

REFLECTIONS AT LORD'S.

I NEVER can walk about Lord's without some such reflections as may be supposed in Rip Van Winkle after his sleep of twenty years: the present and the past come in such vivid contrast before my mind. There is this peculiarity about Lord's as suggestive of such sobering reflections—in other haunts, as in the parks and fashionable promenades, the frequenters change—two or three seasons satisfy the many; but not so at Lord's. Once a cricketer, always a cricketer—as a looker-on at least—is a rule with the fewest possible exceptions. Hundreds do I meet there year after year—men who, if not found at Lord's, you may be sure are not in London, nor even within an easy distance.

There are three favourite matches — the Universities, Gentlemen against the Players, and Eton against Harrow—where we look forward with some confidence to seeing certain old friends whom we never hope to meet elsewhere.

As I walk round the ground I ruminate sometimes on the failing health and the altered figures of men. There is an old chum, who at school rejoiced in the name of Hedge-stake, because he was about the shape of one, now weighs fifteen stone, "larding the lean earth as he walks along." There was the late Sir F. Bathurst, once pointed out to me by Mr. William Ward—as they used to point out Mr. E. H. Budd—as the finest man of his day in combined activity and strength who ever came to Lord's, though later his watch-chain plumbed a perpendicular almost clear of his toes. Then I see gouty men with sticks; and, saddest of all, paralysed men in chairs. Nor can I forget the gradual change time wrought in Lord Frederic Beauclerc. At first I used to see his lordship taking a bat to show some tyro "how fields were won;" then after a few seasons, in which he sat in the pavilion as the Nestor of the M.C.C., he was fond of leaning on some friend's arm, or seeking a sheltered corner and shrinking from every breeze; and last of all he used to appear in his brougham, his health and strength fast failing, with a lady nurse at his side.

Poor Felix died in 1880, in Dorsetshire, having survived his sad attack of paralysis nearly twenty years. I often tried, but never could prevail on him to take my arm; and even "from the loop-hole of his retreat" just to sit still with me, and to criticise and compare play present and past on those fields where once he had been the one man people came to see. "No," he said, "old recollections, and I fear old friends too, will crowd around; the gap is too wide, the fall is too great, it would upset me quite."

Yes, that ring at Lord's shows me every gradation in the scale of life—the once active now stiff and heavy, the youthful grey, the leaders of great elevens passing unrecognised and alone. Every old cricketer knows by sight, and is himself known to, hundreds from frequenting Lord's—people who seem to him as distinct and as peculiar to those haunts as if he returned periodically to another land.

And pass but a few miles off, and see how different are the natives at the Oval. The pavilions differ not more widely in their architecture than in their company. Some few faces are common to both; but there is a City look about the one, and a West-end look about the other. At the Oval, men seem to have rushed away with some zest from their City offices. At Lord's there is a *dilettante* look, as of men whose work, if ever, has yet to come. Even the ring at the Oval and the ring at Lord's have their own decided characters too. The men of labour, no less than the men of leisure, have their style, and in their very cut, and even their very pipes, and in all their toggery, you mark the Surrey-side as distinct from the West-end holiday-maker. And here I do not mean to speak unkindly. Why should not the busy bee be distinct from certain other little creatures that buzz about the human hive?

The first twelve years I knew Lord's, from 1836-1848, Mr. William Ward was a constant attendant and to not a few he represented a bygone generation.

Mr. Ward began to play in 1810, and, unlike Lord Frederic Beauclerc, not only continued the game after the change to round-arm bowling, but Mr. Ward was one of the very few old players who acquitted himself creditably in the new style. The large powerful figure of Mr. Ward, with heavy massive brow, is one never to be erased from the memory of those who knew him. Considering his business habits—a City merchant and Bank of England director, and once an M.P. and not unknown from his speeches in the House—not a few were surprised that such a mind could be so engrossed and so enthusiastically devôted to cricket.

Lord's to Mr. Ward was a British institution. He was as full of the subject of play as it was, and as sanguine and interested as a boy.

By one memorable act of generosity London, and indeed all England, owes much to Mr. Ward. It was Mr. Ward who came forward at a most critical moment and bought the lease of Lord's, and that too at a heavy price, and saved the ground from being long since covered with Corinthian villas. Mr. Ward was an old Wykehamist, and as such was very proud of the achievements of his school; and at his mansion in Bloomsbury-square, a fashionable square in those days, he annually gave a Wykehamist supper, and stood *in loco parentis*, housing the eleven. At this supper he had the good sense to treat boys as boys, and not to spoil their play for the morrow: he gave them sherry-and-water, and nothing stronger. Not so another hospitable gentleman, who, as to the supper, followed Mr. Ward's example. "Here champagne was handed profusely," said my friend, F. Gale, "which I, for one, had positively never tasted before; and the consequence was, that I was found fast asleep at one o'clock in the morning of the second day of the Winchester match, in the middle of St. John's Wood-road, and carried to the station-house as most truly 'drunk and incapable' by Policeman X!" No wonder that after such folly and irregularities in London life, Winchester ceased to put in an appearance at Lord's.

This was the less to be regretted, because they had for some time played at a disadvantage, from the fact that they were more distant from town, and, breaking-up earlier than Eton and Harrow, they could rarely command their best eleven. And till 1850 the Wykehamists had no professional. In that year they were first allowed to hire one, and retained old Lillywhite. Lilly said at once, "You are all for batting. Where's the good of that when you can't bowl, and always have a heavy score against you?" So he taught bowling, and trained a wicket-keeper; and the result was that in 1851 Winchester beat both Eton and Harrow at Lord's, after a long series of defeats.

As to Eton and Harrow also, there was a time when, from extravagant entertainments, and also from "the old fellows" initiating the younger into the mysteries of London life, the head-master of Eton would bear this responsibility no longer, and positively refused to allow his pupils to play at Lord's; and therefore for two years there was no School match at Lord's. At that time I ventured, by request, an article in a newspaper, advising old Etonians to offer to act, like Mr. Ward, *in loco parentis* and ensure the safety of the eleven. Almost immediately such an arrangement was made; but the match is now played before the school breaks up, and all has gone harmoniously ever since.

The School match has from year to year been attended by increasing numbers, till at last, like the University boat race, it has almost merged its original character in the festivities to which it has given rise. It is now a London picnic, an event, like Goodwood, to wait for and prolong the London season. Still, there is some good play to be seen, and above all, an earnestness and soul to win which makes even good judges pleased to look on; and while there is a fair field—though rather circumscribed—and no favour, and the only complaint is that children of an older growth are made as happy as the boys, why should we complain?

Mr. William Ward is chiefly known to the present generation as having made 278 runs, the largest score known in cricket, at least in any match of note. Marsden's innings of 227, in Sheffield and Leicester against Nottingham in 1826, was long deemed a great feat, and compared favourably with Mr. W. Ward's 278 against an eleven decidedly inferior to Marsden's opponents. This score was beaten by Alfred Adams of Saffron Walden, in 1837, who scored 279, one more than Mr. Ward. Adams stood the head of all scores till Mr. Tylecourt scored at Clifton College 402, and Mr. W. G. Grace 400, against twenty-two in the field.

As to the score of Mr. Tylecourt of Clifton College, it was really remarkable, because the two sides were supposed well matched, and he played with worthy compeers. The bowling too was equal to the average of the College bowling on which he had been formed and trained, and the innings extended over several play-hours. This I took the trouble to ascertain, because it had been represented that Mr. Tylecourt's was only a case of the big boy fagging the little ones. It was in reality the fair innings of a schoolboy with respectable school-play.

Mr. Ward's innings was made against Norfolk, by no means a strong eleven, though Mr. E. H. Budd—a man given—bowled. Fuller Pilch, a youth of seventeen, played for Norfolk his first match at Lord's. Mr. Budd told me that Mr. Ward was missed an easy catch before he had scored thirty; but his competitors in long scores no doubt were missed too.

And what style of play was Mr. Ward's? A most efficient style, no doubt, as he scored more in good matches, than any man of his day. One reason was that he cared more about it; he played for his average, or at least for his credit (for averages were less calculated in those days), as well as for the game. Beldham said to me, " As to my score, I could never half play unless runs were wanted, and very few good players ever can." We all know that after seventy or eighty runs, men are often venturesome, and think they have done enough. It required a man of Mr. Ward's cricketing enthusiasm, as well as of his skill, to stand batting into the third day. He was a powerful forward and driving player, with long reach, playing quite upright and straight, and with good judgment. He practised steadily, and made quite a serious business of his practice. His style was very like Tom Hearn's, as Pilch's was like Scotten's, but with much more hitting. "He once," said Caldecourt, "gave me a guinea, because, discovering a weak point in his play, I bowled him out twice one morning." Mr. Ward would also practise at eighteen or nineteen yards, instead of twenty-two, to increase his difficulty. After that he found play at twenty-two yards comparatively easy. Still Mr. Ward was powerful rather than elegant. Lord F. Beauclerc said invidiously, " He was too big to play at Cricket." But as for efficiency, late in life he astonished the Cantabs by the way in which he drove back Mr. Kirwan's swiftest bowling; Mr. Ward, however, well remembered Osbaldeston and Brown, who were even faster still. Mr. Mynn also found in "old Ward" a stubborn and unflinching antagonist.

But of the amateur batsmen of that day, Mr. Charles Taylor was the favourite, with ladies as well as gentlemen. His was an elegant style of play—and, like Mr. A. G. Steel's, it looked like play, and not like a serious and painful operation, as is too common; ladies said he looked so happy with it, so natural and so much at ease. Caldecourt was the first of umpires then, and the very best of cricket tutors; a man of good sense, nor did I ever know a better judge of the game; and Caldecourt used to say that in the style of Mr. Charles Taylor, and in the difference between him and other players, he saw Lord Frederic Beauclerc over again. His lordship stood foremost as a study in Caldecourt's early days, and Mr. Taylor in Caldecourt's later life.

Lord Frederic played for thirty-five seasons, and was good to the last. When fifty-four years of age he scored sixty-five against Ashby, the best bowler of his day. He was one of the most regular attendants at Lord's for sixty years. His son Charles played with me in the first of the University matches, in 1836, and hit a ball which struck above the windows at the public-house, a little higher than a mark which Lord Frederic pointed out as recording a celebrated hit by Mr. E. H. Budd. Lord Frederic was a first-rate match runner, second only to Mr. Budd. A match was one day projected between them, unknown to Mr. Budd, for a heavy stake. "But," said Budd, "I unintentionally marred this by indulging his lordship with a short spin and trial of speed, which convinced him he had no chance."

One curious story of Mr. Ward. On his way to a match in Sussex he lost his watch. A year after, the watch was found in a fagot by a cook while lighting the fire. The fagot proved to have been cut from a hedge over which Mr. Ward had crossed.

The B. matches were curious and notable in the early part of this century—played for twenty-six years. The best players happened to have the initial B to their names: Beldham, Budd, Beauclerc, Beagley, and Bentley were great names indeed. There were also Barton, Bennett, Bridger, Burgoyne, Captain Beckett, Bowyer, Brande, Brown, Broadbridge, Bailey, Burt, Barnett, Sir F. Bathurst, Box, Broughton. The B.s played twelve matches; the first in 1805, the last in 1838. Beagley played in 1816 and 1838, and E. H. Budd in 1805 and 1831.

During all the years of which I am treating, the pavilion—whether at the old ground, the first Lord's, where now is Dorset Square, or at its present site—contained worthy rows of true cricketers, past and present—of true lovers of the game, and of men who, by public-school or University as well as by cricket ties, had that bond of sympathy and fellow-feeling for one joint pursuit which is the *idem velle* and the *idem nolle* not more of Sallust's Roman than of more modern days. To that state I am happy to hear that, from their new system of elections, the Marylebone Cricket Club is in a fair way of fast returning. It is believed that the great responsibilities the members undertook in securing the ground once made them less particular in requiring some cricket qualification in their elections. Money—money, and subscriptions in every form—is a great impediment to the purity of cricket, no less than of more mundane commodities; but happily the present state of the funds of the M.C.C., in spite of their spirited outlay, justifies an independent course, and we once more see this club the most enjoyable summer club society has ever known.

As to gate-money, and playing for the pot, it is cruel to see how it operates in spoiling a match. The first I ever heard of the gate-money interfering with the management of a match was, much to my surprise, at the famous North and South match, when Mr. Mynn was so distinguished at Leicester. The publican told me that he had the privilege of putting the men in, and divided the great batsmen between the two days! Very *infra dig.* for Lord Frederic and the Marylebone Club, by whom it was sanctioned.

Then why do we always have a dinner in the middle of a match? as if players could be worth much after the usual pies and salads, lobsters and custards! Certainly every player can find time for all the luncheon any real cricketer requires; but here again the profit of "the ground" is too often the consideration, and we waste an hour each day. More time in late commencing and loitering is wasted from the same cause. The match seems purposely made to last, to sell beer and to draw sixpences for the third day.

If the game is naturally so long, every means should be taken to save time. But commonly half an hour is wasted before beginning, and half an hour more at luncheon; and if you reckon five minutes for every man who goes in, multiplied by forty for the two innings a side, you have a loss of three hours and twenty minutes more; and to this often we must add half an hour for unnecessary waste of time between the innings. In many matches, especially at the Oval, and wherever the players have an interest in making a three days' match or in playing for a drawn game, from four to five hours that might have been saved are wasted.

Let me suggest a timekeeper, or special instructions to the umpire; also a special agreement between clubs as to time, and the rule that every batsman going in shall meet the batsman coming out.

Nay more; I am credibly informed that in twenty-two matches, and other pothouse fixtures, the object is not to get some great player of the day out, but the contrivance is rather how to keep him in; and some youngster not worth putting up to the secret, who happened to be exulting in a catch that disposed of W. G. Grace was surprised at being far from complimented, but called a goose and a meddler for his pains!

At Lord's, the dinner-time is only half an hour, and time is fairly kept—that is, there is no intentional delay; but at the Oval the matches are far less satisfactory to the lovers of cricket. Even looking to the receipts this is questionable policy. We may be sure that strict play will prove the more attractive in the end, and increase the number of spectators.

All this results from professional cricket and professionals. Professionals are now numerous indeed. To a limited extent they date from an early period. Gentlemen become naturally interested, if not attached to, those who have excited their admiration by their play, rejoiced in the same triumphs, or sympathised in the same defeats. Many an old cricketer in early times ended his days in a keeper's lodge, or held some sinecure on an estate, as did old Fennex at the beautiful gardens of Benhall.

The Duke of Dorset, in the last century, had three professionals, Miller, Minshull, and W.

Bowra, among the best of their day. The Earl of Tankerville had Bedster, and the celebrated Lumpy, so well known to the readers of "Old Nyren." Sir Horace Mann retained George Ring as his huntsman and John Ring as his whipper-in, while Mr. Amherst employed Boxall to bowl to him all the winter in a barn.

But these were feudal times, and such engagements depended on local ties. With cricketers, as with servants, there is naturally little interest on either side where railways whirl attendants perhaps a hundred miles, and master and servant meet as utter strangers to each other. So we have seen painful instances of broken-down professionals, too old for play and never trained to work, friendless and alone.

It is remarkable that no single professional of eminence ever came from Oxford, though Fenner, Buttress, Hayward, Carpenter, and Tarrant remind us of Cambridge practice on Parker's Piece.

It is also observable that over a long series of years scarcely any cricketer of note has ever been numbered with the criminal classes of the country.

As to cricket in foreign parts, the earliest and most remarkable notice of it is found in the *Diary of Henry Teonge, Chaplain on board his Majesty*

Charles II.'s Ships Assistance, Bristol, and Royal Oak, A.D. 1675-1679.

"This morning early, 6th May 1676" (above two hundred years ago), "as is the custom all the summer long, at least forty of the English, with his worship the Consul, rode out of the city" (Antioch) "about four miles, to a fine valley by a river-side, to recreate themselves. There a princely tent was pitched, and we had several pastimes and sports, as duck-hunting, fishing, shooting, hand-ball, *Cricket*, and then a noble dinner, brought thither with great plenty of all sorts of wines, punch, and lemonade; and at six o'clock we returned, all in good order, but soundly tired and weary."

But to come nearer to modern practice, above one hundred years ago we read of an attempt to astonish the natives in France with an All-England Eleven.

The Duke of Dorset was ambassador to France in 1784, and wrote to Yalden, captain of the County Eleven at Chertsey, to select an eleven to go over and show a specimen of the game at Paris. The eleven were got together, and had actually travelled as far as Dover, with the Earl of Tankerville at their head, when they unfortunately met the Duke of Dorset coming home. He was flying before the first outbreak of the French Revolution.

About sixty years passed away, when Mr. Pickering—the gentleman famed as the finest field at cover ever seen, for he could return a ball indifferently as he picked it up right or left—being in the United States, arranged a series of matches with an All-England Eleven.

This eleven was a very powerful one. It comprised Hayward, Carpenter, George Parr, Diver, E. H. Stephenson, Lockyer, Caffyn, Grundy, Wisden, Julius Cæsar, and John Lillywhite Every man could bat well and field well; and though as bowlers there were Jackson, Wisden, Hayward, Caffyn, and Grundy, worthy of any eleven, still Parr's slow bowling proved sometimes more effective still, because, as we have often seen, slows when new are not as easy as they seem.

Soon after, Messrs. Spiers and Pond arranged with the then secretary of the Surrey Club to choose an eleven for a series of matches in Australia, and an eleven not so worthy of England went out, with Griffith, T. Hearne, Roger Iddison, Lawrence, E. Stephenson, Bennett, and Mortlock. A sheriff's officer appeared at the last moment on board at Gravesend, and it was with difficulty that

Mr. Miller, who happened to be present, could collect cash, as cheques were refused, to settle the affair. The man in danger returned with about 400*l.* in pocket from the trip, a lucky hit for a man so impecunious to have missed! This speculation was followed in 1863 by an eleven chosen by George Parr, at that time captain of the Nottingham eleven, with Mr. E. M. Grace, Hayward, Carpenter, Tarrant, Parr, Jackson, R. C. Tinley, Alfred Clarke, Caffyn, Julius Cæsar, Tom Lockyer, and Anderson. This was as good an eleven as to professionals as could be found, save that Daft was conspicuous by his absence.

The first Australian venture had been so remunerative to the contractors, that these players thought they could make better profits in the same way for themselves. But here they were met by a difficulty. The business part of the matter was not so easy to manage in a strange land. Messrs. Spiers and Pond could command the several cricket-grounds, and manage and check the gate-money; and last, not least, could not only advertise with effect, but give *éclat* to their venture, by their knowledge of men and manners, and by their own personal influence.

I was not, therefore, surprised to hear, when a costly grand-stand was required and no one knew whom to trust, that the difference between the attendance and the profits was wide indeed. One of the eleven told me that on one great occasion, when the ground was crowded by thousands, and the grand-stand filled with five-shilling tickets, they were disappointed in their calculations to the extent of 2,000*l*. ! Still the result amply rewarded them for their exertions, and the choice of the eleven gave the greatest satisfaction.

Not so the next eleven, when Messrs. W. G. Grace and G. F. Grace headed a mixed eleven of Players and Gentlemen. The Australians, as predicted by Parr, who formed a high opinion of their promise in 1863, now proved cricketers of no mean reputation. They complained that there was no wicket-keeper worthy the name, and no such bowling as they had seen with Jackson and Tinley. I presume they had learnt slow bowling since they tried Tinley; for Southerton is generally found far more efficient; just as Parr, whose slows were of the most moderate kind, had proved serviceable in America. The names at length were Messrs. W. G. and G. F. Grace, Gilbert, Bush, and Boult ; and as professionals, Jupp, Pooley, Southerton, Oscroft, M. M'Intyre, Andrew Greenwood, and J. Lillywhite. In the play of Messrs. Grace no one could be disappointed, but altogether things did not go well. Painful remarks in the Australian newspapers reached home, naming those whom the colonists did not desire to see again. If the side was weak, strong liquors sometimes made it weaker, and we feared that the game of cricketing in foreign parts was marred for the future.

But not so. Speculators in cricket could discriminate between the abuse and the use of a venture, and contracted for an eleven exclusively professional, as the only means, I presume, of insuring a list of names that had really excited the curiosity and the interest of Sydney or of Melbourne. For such names as Gilbert, Bush, and Boult had not at that time extended their fame to the Antipodes. A stronger side for the out-play could not be found than is implied in the following: Lillywhite (captain), Alfred Shaw, Selby, Jupp, Pooley, Southerton, Emmett, Ulyett, Greenwood, Armitage, Hill, and Charlwood. Here are names most known, and the strongest bowling eleven, but certainly the weakest batting. Sides of twenty-two, by the mere chances of the game, usually make a considerable score; and since they often catch and stop as well as others, I fear that to cut through a crowded field required a little more hitting power than this eleven can display.

Lockwood, Daft, Oscroft, and Shrewsbury are

names we miss; but *linquenda domus et placens uxor*, or, as one of them expressed it, " I would go, only my wife is a married woman, and fears the perils of the sea."

But Australian visits have become common since I wrote of those days.

CHAPTER XXVI.

A TALE OF RUSTICATION.

As to college discipline, it is not very difficult for the college authorities to form an opinion of the character of men, whether idle and throwing time away, or whether they are sensibly availing themselves of academical advantages.

First of all they know the "set" they have joined. The boating set in more colleges than one used to have a bad name, as if rowing and *row*-ing were too nearly allied. My old friend, Harter, of Exeter College, had some difficulty in obtaining the college testimonials, then essential for ordination—a most egregious mistake in his case—chiefly because he was associated with men known to be of by no means a correct character. Men are weighed and considered individually by the tutors over their wine in the Common Room. Few men come up to Oxford quite as strangers; either they or their families are commonly known to one at least of the tutors, as every college has its own connection.

The Common Room conversation is often of this kind: One says—"I am sorry to see Jones has joined Belton's set; his father is anxious about him, and this is a step in the wrong direction." "Yes," says the Dean, "he began by attending morning chapel—no man can be very irregular in his habits while he is up and looks fresh in the morning. Besides, he is in my Gate bill always about the same hour—eleven o'clock." "Then he will soon be known to the proctor," says another, while, perhaps, his tutor adds the information that Jones is less prepared for his lecture than he used to be, and thus the general conclusion is that Jones's career is very unpromising, and that he is on the road to the bad. Add to this, perhaps, duns beset his door; that is known from the scouts. Some tutors make the scouts virtually spies on the men—a class of spies for whom we used to be by no means on our guard, presuming from the fees and perquisites they received from us that they were quite on our side, though we little considered that they had known and received equal indulgences from the said dons for some ten years or more before our time, and were likely to have far more regard to their interest.

My old friend, Joe Wilkinson, had probably been summed up in this way, "especially as his father, an old Trinity man, having himself," said Short, "been once rusticated, had requested particular attention to his son's case." Joe's irregularities and noisy parties in rooms had, at length, become too common to be passed over. So one day the scout came with the usual polite message, "Mr. Short's compliments, and would wish to speak with you at twelve o'clock." Joe came to me and said, "There is a row about something. I am afraid the proctor has been splitting about that affair down in St. Clement's. Just lend me your gown, mine is so tattered and torn, the very look of it proclaims a row-ing man, as the old president told the Count when he snatched his cap from his hand and made a rattle of the broken board." Having put on a decent appearance Joe presented himself to the vice-president.

"Mr. Wilkinson," said Short, "I had rather at all times prevent mischief than punish it. How often have you missed lecture this term?"

"Only twice, sir."

"Only twice, you say. And I suppose it is *only* more times than is creditable that you have missed chapel—that you have had noisy parties, and have knocked in late?"

"Not once after twelve o'clock, sir."

"Yes, but very often after half-past eleven, says

the porter's book. Now I want to impress upon you that in every point you are trying college rules very hard; one step more in the same direction and all your misdoings put together—making up in number what, if anything, they want in excess—will be summed up before the president, in·the Common Room, and then "—here he relaxed, and said, with a good-natured smile—" you will have to retire into 'the bosom of your family,' and I know your father well enough to say a pretty warm reception that will be. Now, I have warned you. My old friend cannot afford to throw away money upon your education, and after all to see you form idle and dissipated habits worse than if you had no college education at all. You may go now; but—take warning."

Exit Joe Wilkinson.

But all this did not avail. " When the wine is in the head the wit is out." Joe fell into the proctor's hands. The attendant on the proctors, whom we knew as " the Marshal," knew by sight nearly every man in the University—certainly every row-ing man in Oxford. Men were much more keenly looked after than they suspected. The jealousy among thieves which betrays many a thief to the policeman is a principle equally powerful among the *pestes noctivagæ*, as a certain proctor denominated them, and no sooner does one of these record a preference than her rival puts the Marshal on the track.

Without entering further into particulars, a proctor once made inquiries at the college as to Joe's usual character. This inquiry revealed enough—though short of proof on which he himself could act—to make the Dons meet in the Common Room; and, after an examination—in which Joe could do nothing but keep silence, look sheepish and let judgment go by default—he was ordered to retire and wait in his room, and soon received a billet in the form following:

"Mr. Wilkinson will leave college before twelve o'clock to-morrow, and not return till next term.
"Common Room, Nov. 5th, 1835."

How far Joe Wilkinson was really affected by this sentence we will not say, but he contrived to put a good face on the matter and to conceal it from his friends. "Never say die," were his first words to me, for I entered soon after the Common Room servant had brought him the sentence. "I have got my walking ticket *et nullus error* (and no mistake)." Phipps and Belton soon joined us. Phipps said: "What a lucky fellow Joe is, to be home just in time for a shot at the pheasants." Charlie said, "I happen to have a supper to-night to a select party, and Wilkinson being, 'as this document witnesseth,' most particularly select in manners and morals both, must join at nine o'clock." But first, a ride across country was proposed, for Wilkinson was to be "kept going and must not be down in the mouth," as the Count said, though more philosophically he might have said, "We must not give him time to think." So, by the help of frequent potations and an unfailing succession of "jolly companions, every one," Joe had little time seriously to realize his position, for egg-flip, bishop and tobacco smoke displaced thought till the time of breaking up, when fatigue —for nothing exhausts more than a sustained struggle between a proud spirit and inward annoyance—we may suppose quickly brought another sedative in the form of sleep; but when Joe awoke next morning—and there is quite enough to account for his awaking somewhat early— surely he must have felt within him a brood of craving thoughts which seemed awake before him, and expecting the moment when memory should arise, refreshed and rife, to minister to their gnawing appetites. Wilkinson, I freely admit, was a lad of a manly spirit, but, being also flesh and blood like other men, he had no more power or control over those inward qualms and hollow sensations than he would have had over a sick head-ache.

However, all this was for a time dispelled by breakfast; for once more a party was made, in compliment to Wilkinson, that his friends might have an opportunity of seeing him off and wishing him good-bye.—And what did we all talk of? Not of the miseries of rustication, you may be sure, but rather of the sport he would be in time for; of his pike fishing, in which he delighted in Iffley Lasher, and then the meets of fox-hounds in his neighbourhood. As for parental displeasure, domestic ties, and family restraints, though there is no one at college who is really insensible of this power, every man seems to think they would be understood by no one but himself, so it was common to hear men speak of what they did at home, as if no one could presume to control or contradict them, and as if each was completely master of his father's establishment.

After breakfast Wilkinson was escorted by the whole party, forming about four strings of three men each, walking arm-in-arm to the Angel, then a principal coach inn, opposite Queen's. Of course the box seat was reserved for Joe; and as the coach started, his friends gave him three cheers, in which the coachmen, porters, and horsekeepers, who perfectly understood the sort of passenger they had taken up, made bold to join.

This was one scene in the drama. Let me now describe another, for, while every hour was bringing Wilkinson nearer home, there was arising a domestic storm with all the conflicting elements of sorrow, anger, indignation, and amazement awaiting the return of the prodigal son, though, unlike the prodigal son in the Gospel, he not only spent his own portion of the family substance, but was, in a fair way to waste a little more still in riotous living.

The Reverend James Wilkinson had no little himself to blame for the blow which that morning fell upon him, and which no little shocked all the rest of the Wilkinson family.

CHAPTER XXVII.

A TALE OF RUSTICATION CONTINUED.

LIFE is self-denial at almost every turn. It is a necessity which increases with our years, because our ties multiply; and "give as well as take" is the condition of all men but of a Robinson Crusoe, before he found his man Friday, on the desert island. But, though life is self-denial, a boy's education—the supposed preparation for this life before him—is too often a training in selfishness and self-indulgence. The sons in a family commonly get everything; the girls come off second best. I have no stronger impression of Oxford life than a certain impression by no means pleasant of men leading a life of luxury out of all proportion to the economy of their families at home, or indeed to the economy to which most must submit when thrown on their own resources. It is at Oxford as elsewhere: some have double the income of others, and consequently set the standard of expense, which the majority find it hard to follow; and I remember a writer in the "Quarterly Review," in reviewing "Peter Priggings," was equally impressed by a recollection of men at college encroaching on the patrimony of their sisters, as well as their own, by their own selfish extravagance; and this selfishness such "Tom and Jerry" views of Oxford life as Peter Priggings, the reviewer justly complained, were but too well calculated to encourage.

Since wisdom in any form is rather a scarce commodity, perhaps we may least expect to find it, however much it may be most wanted, in parents. Parents identify themselves with their sons, and are blinded in their training, not only by affection but by self-love. Still, excuse these infirmities as we will, "as we sow so we must reap." Natural consequences must follow, and parents must rue, either in feeling or in purse, the habits they have been weak enough to encourage, and this we shall find duly exemplified in the case of the now distracted father of our friend Joe.

The Rev. W. Wilkinson, rector of Blankton, was well known to me; and first and last from him, his daughters and his neighbours, I heard a sufficiently detailed account of the way the news of Joe's rustication was received at the Rectory.

If there is any one subject of which neighbours, proud of their own sons' doings, are likely to hear rather more than they like, it is the incessant topic of "my son Joe." Parents are fond enough of talking of their own sons, but listen with far more jealousy than interest to the sayings and doings of the precocious progeny of others, while at the same time to the scrapes and failures of those sons they lend a ready ear. To hear that old So-and-So, who is always making such a boast and such a fool of his boy, has found at last that the said prodigy is neither better nor wiser than other young scamps—this piece of news is greeted as nuts by all the rival parents in the neighbourhood. This jealousy especially prevailed in Blankton in regard to Mr. Wilkinson's son Joe.

Joe was a fine, spirited fellow, and a great favourite with both high and low all the country round. He was first in the Blankton Cricket Club, and, whether in rabbiting, riding, or fishing, he could take the shine out of nearly all the youths thereabouts, and thereby, of course, he excited the jealousy of their papas and mammas. If there was a warren to be netted, a colony of rats to be ferreted, or even a pig to be killed, every farmer would gladly have notice given to Master Joseph.

Unfortunately men who take the lead at home cannot endure to play second at college, where all eminence but of a literary kind costs money; so the rector had more than once found that he had been encouraging habits for which he had to pay.

In this position of affairs, and when every letter with an Oxford postmark was enough to spoil the rector's appetite for his breakfast, there came one with a big seal, which was nervously cut open and read, rather to the terror of the wife and daughters, who, in the arched eyebrows and lengthened face of the reader, descried unutterable things.

"What does this mean?" exclaimed Mr. Wilkinson, throwing the letter down on the table. "Some mischief, certainly. Joseph not to keep next term and lose this! Midnight uproar—waste of time—can't be passed over—as a bad example! Very sorry. Hope for amendment for the future. Sentence of 'rustication.'

"Rustication! What's rustication?"

Joe had often spoken of men being "spun," and of "having a walking ticket," but the word rustication was wholly new to Mr. Wilkinson, who had graduated not at Oxford, but at Dublin.

"Oh!" said one of the girls, who had just read

a letter from Joe. "It is not much—nothing poor Joe could help. Some men got tipsy in Joseph's party. He could not give up the names, so the penalty has fallen on him. Poor Joe! I am sure he could not help it."

The father became very violent and furious. "Disgrace of some kind, that is very evident. The term lost too! More loss of time and money both! I wonder where my expenses and repeated anxieties about this boy are to end?"

"*Quicquid delirant reges flectuntur Achivi.*" In other words, when the father of the family is in a rage, woe be to the poor mother and daughters. All their endeavours to explain or excuse Joseph from his own account of the matter served only to intensify the father's anger.

An angry man will pace the room. It is nature's alleviation for excitement of the brain. No wonder, therefore, that the father, after a very bad quarter of an hour for himself and household, took his hat and sallied out.

He had not gone far before he met the squire, whose son was dull and heavy, called steady, one of those youths who rarely went wrong, because there was no go in him at all. The rector was walking so fast, swaying his stick and otherwise giving vent to his peccant humours with such symptoms of agitation, that the squire stood still, prepared for that kind of explosion for which his friend was rather noted in the parish. Well, out it came:

"I am altogether dumbfounded—a letter from Oxford this morning—from the vice-president of Trinity—my son's college—he has done something or other—something 'refractory,' I suppose, as they say at the workhouse. And—but do you know what rustic—rustication means?"

"Oh, yes," said the squire, inwardly chuckling at the opportunity of paying off his neighbour for setting up his own son over the sons of all the fathers in the parish. "I will explain it to you in a moment. Pray, how much does this term cost you?"

"Sixty or seventy pounds."

"Well, then, you will have to pay that over again, for this term counts for nothing. But take my advice. Go to the root of the matter. Rustication does not imply very correct behaviour, of course, and, while good ways are always cheap, bad ways, especially at college, are always dear. Catcham the lawyer is your man. Set him to work, as Captain Passmore did the other day. Young Passmore—you heard of his scrape—confessed he might owe three hundred pounds, so Catcham provided for seven hundred, as a reasonable margin, and what do you think that boy's extravagance amounted to in unpaid bills?"

Mr. Wilkinson looked blank.

"Why, eleven hundred pounds, and a little over!"

Oh, Mr. Wilkinson; you committed a sad mistake indeed for a man who pretends to know the ways of this wicked world! You should never seek to ease your mind by letting your neighbours know of your misfortunes.—By the evening of that day every man, woman, and child in the parish of Blankton had added one new word to their vocabulary, and that new word was "rustication."

As to the Wilkinson household, I pitied them. "I never heard master talk so rough before," said the gardener; and the parlourmaid said it was "a heartache to see missus. What had Master Joseph done, surely he hadn't robbed anyone or took to stealing?" for this was the only kind of evil-doing very familiar to her mind.

"It must be bad—something very bad," was the general presumption. "Rustication was only another word for expulsion and disgrace and ruin for life."

It is evident, therefore, that, both within doors and without, anything but a pleasant reception awaited our poor friend Joe.

To return to Joe. After the excitement of his friendly parting, no doubt, when left to himself and his own cool meditations on the top of the coach, there came reaction, and no very pleasant anticipations of what awaited him at home. Probably, the nearer he drew to the end of his journey the more cigars he smoked, and the more he "liquored up" while changing horses. And it is only of probabilities I can speak as to the state in which he found his father and all the family. Most probably his mother met him sadly and sorrowfully at the door, and then his sisters crept out one by one into the passage. Perhaps his father did not come out to meet him at all, but remained sitting with his feet in the fender, and the back of his chair to the door. We may naturally suppose that there was a secret contest between them as to who should approach the all-engrossing subject first. Homer describes a gentleman who, when a guest paid him a visit, entertained him handsomely nine whole days, and did not speak a word about the special business till the tenth. Homer also specifies that they had plenty, but not variety—

good ox-beef, and abundance of it, day after day, and fresh killed, too. They did not hang their beef, it seems, in those days, though we read of it salted for the sailors, for whom, by the way, an expression very like "old salts" was the characteristic term. I am afraid that Mr. Wilkinson and his son talked over the matter in hand a little sooner, but I pass on to more authentic history.

"If my father will be so absurd, and likes to persevere in being so silent and grumpy, it is not my fault. He can write to Isaac Williams, and he will, I am sure, repeat the same words with which he parted from me—that they did not mean to accuse me of anything disgraceful; but for those noisy parties they must hold the host answerable; and these disturbances had been so frequent that college discipline required an example."

When Isaac Williams so expressed himself, he was somewhat softened by an observation made by Joe to the effect that all he had to say about the sentence of the Common Room was that he wished it had been something to fall more directly on himself, and not of a kind to grieve and alarm his friends.

These good traits were never lost on so excellent a creature as was Isaac Williams.

But it is no use talking, Joe; you don't understand matters. Will all this reasoning spare your father's pocket or his pride? What kind of return can he now expect in any improvement on your part for all the money he is spending on your supposed education? What has become of all his boasting of "his boy at Trinity?" and how is he to stand the sneers of his jealous neighbours, Stanley, Wilton and Co.? And what an example to your younger brother! And what will all the parish say, who think it only a new-fangled term for expulsion? " Why, expulsion in my day," said one old gentleman, " used to mean being flogged and turned out, so that a lad could not enter any profession, and was considered disgraced and ruined for life."

Soon people began to ask who would officiate for Mr. Wilkinson the next Sunday. No one could imagine that their pastor could have the nerve to appear before his people for some weeks after so vital a stab to the respectability of his family.

While the younger brother is executing some little commission in the village, Mr. Wandle, who sells brooms, mops, starch, treacle, and something of all sorts, and is churchwarden besides, sounds Master Charles as to whether the report is true that he must qualify for the family living, " as people say that after this unlucky business Mr. Joseph can never take holy orders, though one would hope it was not so bad as that."

"These everlasting blunders"—such were the words in which poor Joe's indignation found vent —"and all this nonsense, as if anybody cared for the opinions of such a scrubby set of people as those of Blankton—is most disgusting. Why, the dons themselves, as my scout has whispered to me, have had row-ing parties, too, in their undergraduate days, and fallen into the proctor's hands, too. So what do I care for the opinion or verdict of a set of old, fusty dons in a Common Room, as proud of their 'little brief authority' as if they were so many lord-chancellors?"

Such were the daily and hourly outpourings of poor Joe—always vowing he did not care, but always with his back up, and feeling like a young Atlas, with the whole world—that is, the whole of the little world of Blankton—as a very heavy weight upon his shoulders. Oh, Joseph, Joseph! be patient, and submit to your punishment. All this exaggeration and scandal is part and parcel of it. Go where you will, you will find Blankton people to taunt, to gossip, to exaggerate, and to misrepresent.

The loss of a term may make a material difference to some men. After rustication I have known testimonials for holy orders refused or suspended, and every old Oxonian knows that no man is rusticated unless generally known to be leading a life wholly inconsistent with that improvement which academical advantages should imply.

That "misfortunes do not come singly" is true indeed, in the sense that evil breaks out in more ways than one. If Joe was doing little good at college, he needs must have been doing some mischief, for man is a piece of machinery which must operate on something.

One morning a bill came in. The letter was hastily opened by the father before he saw it was directed to his son. It was a bill of forty pounds for Seckham's gig, lately smashed! Here was a blow indeed; for there had been no little domestic disturbance about Joe's debts, and he was not supposed to indulge in horses.

Just about this time, as a salutary diversion, an old Oxonian, a wild boy in his day, and thence the better able to understand and make the best of things, was on a visit near Blankton, and called and gave a little sensible advice to Mr. Wilkinson. "It is but too true," said he, "that every father accuses everybody's son of leading his own son astray. Still, it is so far true in your son's case, that I believe he would do very well but for the fast set he has joined. Now, in twelve months nearly all of those men will have left; so, if time is no object, let him read with some poor curate hereabouts for a year. He has been talking to me and things are better than they seem, and the sooner you make this affair up with him the better. How was it that you did not know that when a youth at college asks for such sums as he has, he owes three or four times that amount? Your last remittance, it seems, he honestly paid away in debts, but this particular debt came in later. Make allowance; you can't have—few, at least, can—sons arrived at that particular crisis and age of *in*-discretion at which they all come to, without the bother of them. If fathers will leave their sons, for two or three years together, in the management of as many hundreds a year as they before had pounds, and leave them without any check, inquiry, or guidance, they must expect to suffer for it. I will venture to say, Wilkinson, that with all your experience, last Christmas you found you had taken too sanguine a view of your own liabilities?"

Mr. Wilkinson looked guilty.

Let us change the scene. Let us consider that thirty years had passed away, and the poor father and his troubles had passed away too. Joe, now grey-headed, had sent one son to Trinity. We talked and laughed over the past. "An old poacher makes the best gamekeeper," said Joe; "remembering my long-suffering father, I acted on our old friend's advice, and though I had some tics to pay, I kept expenses within bounds, and had not so much to complain of."

CHAPTER XXVIII.

A SURVEY OF UNIVERSITY ADVANTAGES.

Now let us sum up all the distinctive advantages of a University education—the influences for good, which I sensibly felt, not forgetting also the influences for evil prevailing elsewhere, from which I was spared for three years of the most impressionable season of my life. Impressionable! —yes, most truly so. Horace, in his character of youth, says, "Like wax for taking evil impressions."

First of all, I was removed from my native town and its limited circle of youthful companions, amongst whom it was easy to stand first, and most natural for my family, as for myself, to think me better than I was. At Oxford the whole scene was changed. I felt one of many, and a very insignificant unit too. I felt conjured, as it were, from the top of the class at home into a new school, to begin almost at the bottom; the change to me was wonderful. I was like "the new boy," to work my way up. I was last in choice of rooms, I was at the bottom of the freshmen's table in hall, I was placed in the easiest lecture, yclept by Count Wratislaw, "The heavy Euripides." My whole surroundings were so different. The whole scene was changed. Whoever saw so many men of about the same age brought together before! At once I was in a wider sphere. Everything, bad as well as good, I am sorry to confess, was on a larger scale too. Without boasting of exceeding innocence, I was surprised to find what apt scholars in the school of vice, knowing "how to commit the oldest sins the newest kind of ways," could come together from the public schools. A freshman's set is generally the worst, as the better class of men at Oxford, as elsewhere, are guarded in forming new acquaintances. Eton, Harrow, Winchester, and Westminster having all large numbers, the variety of characters good and evil in each are large in proportion. Any one who listened to their confessions would be prepared to learn henceforth what a strange menagerie, "clean beasts by twos and unclean beasts by sevens," was the wide world he was about to enter, if at least what he here saw was a fair sample of it.

How much better the worst part of public schools may be now, I cannot say. I am speaking, be it remembered, of my experience fifty years since, at which time, Stanley says, Arnold had no little vice to contend with at Rugby. In one place he says that Arnold could not look without painful feelings at a cluster of big boys over the fire together, fancying that he saw the very spirit of the Evil One brooding among them.

But some one will say—Was this knowledge advantageous? There was at least so much compensation, that to know this world we must know all grades and classes, the nature of the evil to avoid as well as the good to ensue.

But such painful studies of character are limited. It was not long before I was able to leave these dregs of society to their own corruption, and to find no little of a pleasant and improving kind. In this society I soon observed that the standard of superiority at Oxford was very different from that of my father's social circle of older persons. Here there was no longer some Sir Wormwood Scrubs, or some brainless landlord of five-hundred acres, or some other Golden Calf to claim our worship. It was no longer the money, but the man. It was Roundell Palmer who had won the Ireland Scholarship and other prizes; Rickards and Thomas, prizemen also; or, in another line, Gladstone, Lowe, or Sidney

Herbert leading at the Union; Pelham and Copleston in their racing boats; or Wordsworth, Wright, and Popham on the Cowley cricket ground; or perhaps Crawley Boevey, then the best man at a steeplechase. Even idle men spoke with some fire of emulation of men who had in these ways done credit to their college, and few could look without respect to the Scholars' table or refuse to acknowledge men thus proved superior to themselves. At once I began to feel smaller, very low down in this very large class, and that I must do a great deal if I ever hoped to rise in it. My proper place and rank in this new society was no longer to be mistaken. I sensibly felt, "These are no flatterers, but feelingly remind me what I am."

Nor was it long before a decided change took place in my estimation of my private school education and the comparative advantages of others. It happened that one day after lecture my old friend Joe Walsham proposed a little reading together. Joe was one of Dr. Butler's scholars from Shrewsbury. This revealed to me early advantages of which I had never an idea. My time had been spent among third-rate scholars and dissipated among a number of so-called modern subjects, whereas Joe and his schoolfellows had been so taught classics that most of these subjects became easy, and took care of themselves. He soon detected my special deficiencies, scratched off from my list of subjects the least important, and set me reading with more interest and to some purpose.

Once more, and in the field of literature, my new world seemed bigger and myself smaller, and I was beginning to find my place in it. A great point is gained in education when you know what others know—what is really practicable and how high to aim with some chance of hitting your mark. For want of this self-knowledge we daily see men starting for prizes in this race of life with a small chance of reaching the proposed journey's end, reminding us of Virgil's *Italiam Fugientem*— the longer they run the further they are off. Not long since I heard a clever, but self-taught, man propound in a lecture the most common-place decisions as new and original, all because he had never measured himself with others, as at college, and wholly mistook the standard of a literary audience.

To the same point of valuable self-knowledge and experience in men and manners all the little incidents and peculiar habits of college life served to tend.

About eight o'clock every day there was a very general assembling from every staircase, as if nearly all the college were pouring forth together, for morning chapel. Eight attendances a week were the rule, and most preferred the morning service, as least likely to interrupt either the boating or the cricket, at four p.m. in the summer, or the wine parties at seven p.m. in the winter. After morning chapel we had a short lecture in hall either in Latin or in Divinity, and generally "send your commons to my room" was a friendly invitation to club our bread and butter for breakfast, your friend supplying the tea, coffee, and eggs, &c. There were also "breakfast coaches," where half-a-dozen men of congenial spirit supplied in some simple way the breakfast in turns. My breakfast coach once consisted of a national variety. There was Jones, from Wales; Pat Baker, from Ireland; Macgregor, from Scotland; and Preston, from the Land's End in Cornwall, with Charlie, before introduced to the reader.

Of course—as the saying that "man never continueth in one stay" is even more true and descriptive of college than of life in general—these were in the course of my terms replaced by others; but this will suffice to show the varied experience and the collective experience of college life—making a man, even in his early days, a citizen of the wide world instead of his ideas being limited by the latitude and longitude of the paternal parish alone, where, as in the proverb, "Home birds have home-spun ideas," and cannot possibly have much more. The least consideration will show that the Keble College sytem of all meals in the common-hall, however economical, is socially by no means so advantageous.

The choice which college life affords of a large number of companions, whether for boating, cricket, or other amusements, evidently conduces to the same wide experience of men and manners. And as to classical studies, is there nothing in the very *genius loci*—in associations with the scenes of the studies of great men departed, and with the time-honoured institutions of the place? Is there nothing in the very name of Oxford? I ask this in the spirit of Charles Lamb, who said: "Is there nothing to conjure up a spirit in the name of Rome more than in the name of Romford?" Why do men agree in sending their sons to France or Germany for learning foreign languages? Surely they could find Frenchmen and Germans to converse with their sons at home? Very true. But experience shows that the result is different. There is something in this foreign atmosphere and surroundings which creates an interest and gives a stimulus which you miss at home. This is true of Oxford studies. These were something, if we regarded only the seclusion from domestic interruption. Old Dr. Symons, of Wadham—" Big Ben," or " Benjamin the ruler "—said to my friend Jeans when he spoke of long vacation studies, "Are there any women in your house?" "Yes, sir; my mother and three sisters." "Then I am afraid you won't read much. I don't believe in study when there are women in a house. No, no; you won't read much there."

I agree, therefore, you may have Oxford tutors, with money at command, at home, but the result generally would not be the same. You would miss the emulation, and a certain sympathy and interest in classical studies, which prevails at Oxford, and which each recurring season keep present to the mind. Every spring and autumn we have "greats," and with these the constant talk of more promising candidates and of the expected style of examination.

Then reading men went to listen in the schools, and returned full of the questions asked and the apt answers given, and sometimes the strange misconstruings of the candidates, of which last I remember one rather strange instance as from an Ireland scholar, who translated *malis ridentem alienis,* " laughing at his neighbour's misfortunes," not seeing that the long *a* in *malis* implied not misfortunes, but cheeks. There was always much emulation as to honours and classes among the men of different colleges, and always a question as to whether the Ireland scholar would come out in the first class; for in two instances with the Shrewsbury scholars there were notable failures. "No," said Short, "do not expect it. The system is bad with Dr. Butler's men; they make an early show with scholarships by the exercise of their memories, but they have never learnt to think, and therefore break down in the schools."

The daily lectures, in which we could not fail to measure ourselves with the best men of the colleges, some of them now the best men of the day, I have always felt a great advantage, not only because we saw what they could do, but also because I feel that I know more nearly than otherwise I could know what they could not do, and therefore the limits of human powers and understanding.

No doubt many a lecture did seem at the time worth very little, when I happened to be well acquainted with the subject of it, and because lectures were always at that hour in the morning when I was most eager to read. But that was unavoidable; lectures were most beneficial on the balance both socially and intellectually.

In speaking of University advantages, I would be understood to explain that it was not in one but in a combination of many influences mentioned that this benefit consists; for many little points must concur to determine social advantages of any kind.

Again, all that is good and generous in youth is at Oxford for the time unalloyed by the sordid and money-getting cares of life. Men meet at college to improve not their circumstances but themselves. Some, it is true, are said to "read for the pot," for the return in pupils or fellowships they may obtain—suing the Muses, like other ladies, rather for their fortunes than their charms. But those called "smugs" formed a small proportion, and are hardly to be counted against the usual disinterestedness of Oxford students.

Nor, in estimating the benefits of Oxford, must we fail to observe that we must not only consider the good that there ensues, but the evil elsewhere that we avoid; an advantage which may fairly be set down in favour of a university education. Suppose the case of a youth who has to pass his time from the eighteenth to the twenty-first year of his age in idleness at home, and as yet in no profession. Any man of the world would say that he was probably on the road to ruin, in mind, body and estate, unless he had the rare resources of one youth in twenty. "There goes young So-and-so," is the remark, "ringing the changes of amusement outdoor and within, palled with satiety of balls and dissipations various." Of course all pleasure soon results in no pleasure. As our taste palls for the dainties, so the interest flags for the sport. When the gentleman depends on his gun or his boat to get an appetite for his dinner, as much as the gamekeeper or the boatman to get a dinner for his appetite, the latter has the advantage of the two; for where he retires to grateful ease after his labours, his master dreads a return of vacuity and *ennui*. Besides, there is an instinct and a conscience to be useful. The mere idler can hardly look a man of sense and energy in the face. Of course there are busybodies everywhere to remind him that they expect him to be doing something like other people, so he meets more coolness than sympathy wherever he goes.

Again, suppose at the age for college, the youth enters any office or house of business, what manner of men will be his companions, to form the style or the sentiments of the future man? If every college, as I have said, marks its own hue, tone and complexion on its students, in this season so critical for the morals and the refinement of every man, what sort of models will surround him now? Think of the low clerks and vulgar people to whom in business a large part of your time must be daily devoted; think of the chicanery, the quibbling, the shuffling with which, be he ever so honest, the sharp wit and blunt conscience of the litigious must tend to familiarize him. What shall we say of the sordid, the vindictive, and the selfish feelings with which a mind yet pure and unsuspecting is to be made prematurely conversant? Then a knowledge of the ways of the world, of human nature, shrewdness, wariness, and caution, are certain qualifications of a very mixed and alloyed character, and rather dangerous for youth to learn. Who is there that would not fear that three years of influence so baneful, and of intercourse so chilling, might be fatal to that sentiment of honour and generosity which is the pride and ornament of manhood!

But as to the mind also, consider how much will be lost by this beginning of life? All previous instruction, even in the best of schools, will be stopped at the very point at which it begins to be serviceable. Improving studies are closed for ever. The newspaper, the novel, and the magazine, for the most part, mark the extent of his reading and the depths of his understanding for life.

Believe me, I have seen the two systems of university training and the habits formed in business : I have been able to compare the result in two brothers, side by side; the difference was remarkable. You would hardly believe they were the sons of the same parents, or the formation of the same social state.

"The real nature of collegiate studies," says an elegant writer, " is still as little known by the generality as it was a hundred years ago. Not one in fifty, even, of those who have profited by them, could give the true reasons of their excellence. University studies are but a small part of collegiate education. Professors or lecturers may form the scholar; they cannot make the man. It is in this formation of character—a higher aim surely than any mere scientific attainments—that our universities and public schools must take their stand. The best of all knowledge, self-knowledge, is the staple they impart. A man educated in it rarely mistakes his own position or feels uneasy in it." So true is this, that I have often heard men say "This is beyond me, I cannot go the pace. I was in the fifth form at Eton and learnt then that too many could give me the go-by."

But I could name one, who, looking back on college days past, could sum up most of his advantages, and say "Oh, for the days when I had rooms to myself, with an oak to shut intruders out, the college library for reference, and lectures on all I wanted or was good for me to read." Then there were examinations and class-lists always coming or expected, literary men to converse with, the latest news, the answer or the failings of class-men, successful or disappointed, as the talk of every dinner table; not to mention the easiest ways to do the hardest work, and rumoured crotchets and new examiners, told by some man who heard it of some one else, who heard it at a tutor's breakfast—reports which give such a timely fillip to a reading man, who is beginning to knock up. When all these stimulating influences were in the air I breathed and the sphere in which I moved, whom can I blame but myself if I threw such opportunities away?

Then there were those awe-inspiring, and most admonitory buildings of the place, the Schools for Examination, that seemed to lie in my direct way to and from every place. Oh! who can pass them and see that door by which so many a poor fellow with white tie and bands has gone in trembling, come out sanguine, and been ready to sink again from excitement, as he waited to read his fate in the class-lists yet wet from the examiner's pen! Oh! those Schools, and that classic walk contiguous, with such unclassic name, yclept "the Pig Market." "Who that," as Falstaff said, "had a heart in his belly bigger than a pin's head," could ever look around as he passed that square and not feel the place admonitory indeed? Old Orpheus' vocal notes were as nothing to those placarded, those dismal-looking, doors. Oh, what a sinking, what a sense of a certain vacuum by nature most abhorred, have I felt as I crossed that court, and stood and pondered on what would be the feelings with which I should go in, come out, and wait for testamur or class paper, when a few short terms had passed away!

Then to view the countless volumes of the Bodleian—to study the marbles, the pictures, the curious relics of Tradescant, of Ashmole, the modern contributors of the Duncan's—to read the many notices that overlay the walls of the Schools, of lectures and readings by noted men on every tongue, from Sanscrit to Anglo-Saxon, and on every subject, from pastoral theology to agricultural chemistry, is enough to overwhelm, by the embarrassment of its riches, the zeal of the most promising and ardent student.

Walk where you will in Oxford there are countless associations to turn your thoughts : the quadrangle of Wolsey, the cloisters of Laud, the walk of Addison, and the rooms of Johnson, proclaim a severe and long-tried system, whose fruits have more than answered in richness, though they differ in kind, from the expectations of the founders.

CHAPTER XXIX.

INFLUENCES, SOCIAL AND LOCAL, AT OXFORD.

To look back over college days makes a man for a moment pensive, if not melancholy. It is a little life in miniature. It has its dawn, its noon-day, and its night; its youth, its manhood, and its age; first proud self-complaisance, with warm and sanguine hopes, as of days too many to count; of strength, vigour, and resolution, too rife to fail; then a more subdued and tempered season, with schemes more moderate for greater safety; the first dawn of suspicion and distrust in itself and others; and at last the autumn and the harvest—when the work of spring is done, or closed, at last, irrevocably, and when the wise may exult as they reap, but the foolish must sigh for the days when they were too thoughtless or too confident to till or to sow.

As to the social intercourse of college, everything which happens, from the rustication of some fast man to the installation of a Chancellor, from the winning of a cricket match to the last Ireland Scholarship, or expected double first-class in the Schools, all these matters soon spread; every college is soon well informed of what is notable in any other. If there was any state trial or political crisis, or anything new expected in the literary world, then there was always a Sugden, Denman, or Peel in one college, or a Scott, Wilberforce, or Lockhart, or if not, a nephew or cousin, at least, of Southey, Moore, or Rogers in another, or at least some man who knew someone else who had given him the last news of Abbotsford or Brentwood. And then how grateful is the importance of being purveyor of these state secrets, or Parnassian mysteries. Then with what interest do we read the same speech in Thucydides, or the same chorus of Æschylus, as that in which the best man of the day was examined the morning before.

What is the mere parochial gossip of our vacation compared with the breadth of information and the stirring interests of a university breakfast or wine party? The one is limited almost to the bounds of a single parish; the other is enriched with the tributary streams of daily history from every quarter of the British Empire. And what is your vacation society, too? Where but in one of our universities can you, any stated morning, meet ten or fifteen young men together, all accustomed only to the best society, and with minds yet untainted by the selfishness, the jealousies, the contentions, and animosities which the daily struggle for daily bread, the galling compromises of an independent spirit, and all the " contumely which the deserving from the unworthy take," insensibly imprint upon the heart, blunting the fine-edged true nobility and marring the delicate sensibility of the man? No, no. Few men are blessed with the chastening influence of this society after academic days.

But be it remembered that to enjoy these benefits a youth must be placed in a fair position to take full advantage of this social as well as intellectual sphere. Yes. It is quite possible to be in Oxford and not of it. Some have no higher aim in sending their sons to college than to profit by the endowments, to qualify with the name of B.A. or M.A.—a mere speculation of business, perhaps to add to a Prospectus for a would-be schoolmaster. This, though not unknown at Oxford, is far more common at Cambridge. A friend who migrated from Cambridge, after six terms spent there, to Oxford, remarked to me that the difference which struck him was especially this:

at Cambridge he felt in a place of business, while it was purely education at Oxford.

This is well explained by Mr. Stedman, in his excellent guide to college, called "Oxford: its Social and Intellectual Life." I agree with him that for a real university education a parent must be prepared to spend about £75 on rooms, fees, and preliminary expenses, and not less than £220 a year afterwards. From £850 to £1,000 for the expenses total from the matriculation to the degree, including private "coaching"—required if a man reads for honours—is a fair and not an extravagant estimate. To live as a gentleman no man should be prepared with less.

It is sometimes said that a man with proper care and economy may live at a college for £140 a year, the year academical being only six months; and graduate for £400 in all.

No doubt he can do so; but this will be Oxford with all the best part of Oxford left out. He may stint himself to the plainest meals, though here I don't pity him, but he must not spend a penny for wines or entertainments of any kind. He must have a tailor's bill at which a poor clerk would smile. By refusing to subscribe to college clubs, and withdrawing himself from the society of his equals; by borrowing his neighbour's books and his neighbour's spoons, he must lead the life of a smug! This is not an exaggerated picture of the life of many, of too many, undergraduates. And what a contrast this is to the bright picture a young man naturally forms of a university life. Such a poor fellow is obliged to decline hospitality, for his proper pride will not allow him to accept that which he knows his humble means do not enable him to return. He refuses to row, for he cannot afford the subscriptions; he will not be able to take his place in his college eight-oar or Torpid, because the incidental expenses will be too great for his scanty allowance.

An undergraduate will generally feel obliged to subscribe to college clubs, and should, if not too poor, make it a point of honour to support such institutions; for an ordinary college owes in a great degree its reputation to the position it takes on the river and in the cricket-field, and this must fail unless its clubs are properly supported. We confess there is often an excessive amount of moral pressure applied for the purpose to men unfortunately who are really unable to subscribe, but whose poverty is held to be a mere pretence. Such men are in a cruel position—a fact which parents would do well to consider. A poor fellow in this false position must seek the society of men poor and cramped like himself, or perhaps, in lieu of such, prefer his own; his temper becomes soured, and the man who came to Oxford with bright and pleasant hopes retires thence anything but a grateful son, with no happy memories to cheer him, and it may be with a moroseness which will cling to him throughout his life.

Such men had better pursue their studies at home. The degree they take is a mere ticket to impose on society at large, for of academical training and influences they have little indeed.

The *genius loci* of Oxford surpasses that of every town in England. It were hard to pass three years there without some humanising influence of those grey walls which speak of mediæval times and solemn associations with a long series of great men who have made it the early sojourn in their mortal pilgrimage, great men who have passed away, but not without leaving great works to represent them, most truly " footprints on the sands of Time."

Let us take a walk among the colleges in the order of foundation.

The thirteenth century has given us besides St. Mary's three colleges :

1. University College, then restored, though said to date from Alfred the Great. Here studied Bishop Ridley, Lords Eldon and Howell.

2. Balliol, the college of Robert Southey and Adam Smith.

3. Merton, the college of Bishops Hooper and Jewell, Wickliff, and Dr. Harvey (the discoverer of the circulation of the blood).

The fourteenth century has left us four colleges:

1. Exeter, the college of Samuel Wesley, Froude, and Lord Coleridge.

2. Oriel, the college of Bishop Kerr, Sir Walter Raleigh, Pusey, Keble, Newman, and Archbishop Whateley.

3. Queen's, the college of the "Black Prince," Henry V., Cardinal Beaufort, and Wycherley.

4. New College, famed for the education of William Pitt and Sydney Smith.

The fifteenth century has given us three colleges:

1. Lincoln, the college of Sir W. Davenant and John Wesley.

2. All Souls, the college of Jeremy Taylor, Blackstone, and Sir Christopher Wren.

3. Magdalen, the college of Cardinal Wolsey, John Hampden, Addison, and Gibbon.

The sixteenth century has given us six colleges:

1. Brasenose, the college of Ashmole, of Burton, author of "The Anatomy of Melancholy," and Reginald Heber.

2. Corpus, the college of Keble and John Conington. It was founded by Richard Fox, Bishop of Winchester.

3. Christchurch, founded by Cardinal Wolsey, the college of Wellington, Canning, Peel, Gladstone, William Penn, John Locke, Ben Jonson, and Charles Wesley.

4. Trinity, the college of Lord North, Earl of Chatham, Walter Savage Landor, Cardinal Newman, and Lord Selborne.

5. St. John's, connected with Merchant Taylors' School by twenty-one scholarships, held at £100 a year for seven years. This was the college of Archbishops Laud and Laxton.

6. Jesus College, founded by Queen Elizabeth, at the suggestion of Hugh Price, especially as a place of education for Welshmen.

The seventeenth century has given us two colleges:

1. Wadham, the college of Sir Christopher Wren, Admiral Blake, Lord Westbury, and Dr. Bentley, who, though a Cambridge man, was M.A. of Wadham.

2. Pembroke, the college of Bishop Bonner,

John Pym, Beaumont, Blackstone, George Whitfield, Sir Thomas Browne, Dr. Johnson and the late Bishop Jackson.

In the eighteenth century we have one college only:

1. Worcester, the college of Lovelace, De Quincey, Sir Kenelm Digby, and Foote.

In the present century we have Keble College and Hertford College. The history of this latter is curious. In the thirteenth century Hertford Hall was founded, and in 1740 incorporated as Hertford College, but from want of sufficient endowments the college was dissolved in 1805, part of the college property being appropriated to the Hertford scholarship, and part transferred to Magdalen Hall, a hall subsidiary to the Magdalen College. In 1874, by Act of Parliament, Magdalen Hall was dissolved, and its members were incorporated as Hertford College. Famous members of this college have been Hobbes, Tyndale, Lord Clarendon, C. J. Fox, Selden, and Dean Swift.

These are indeed subjects for reflection as we wander about this city of colleges. A man must be miserable indeed who can live without improvement in taste and feeling amidst so much architectural beauty and such inspiring associations.

As to natural beauty, the Christ Church meadow, with the Isis and the Cherwell, and the gardens of Magdalen and New College especially, where the richest verdure blends with the grey antiquity of the buildings—this it were hard to find elsewhere. Here we have " sermons in stones and good in everything."

Oxford, like a large school, a school for adults, is a little world—a stage for rehearsals, and where errors are comparatively harmless, before we encounter a more censorious audience in the drama of life. As we move up term by term from the lowest table to the highest in our college hall, from the days of our freshman's study to our final examination, we seem to have passed from youth to maturity. It is a sphere to rectify our illicit spirits and then clarify our judgment of men and manners. We learn while walking through the crowd of life neither to run against any one nor to let any one run against us. We are taught to feel our way with our neighbour's prejudices—to watch the cloud on an angry brow, to say enough and not too much—there is no mercy for presumption or for prosing—to treat kindly and tenderly those little failings and conceits which make up the compound man.

Charles Lamb spoke of men of imperfect

sympathies: he means men who work not glibly and smoothly in the machinery of life, more like the grit than the oil in the social wheel—men of repulsive attraction—men who, in conversation, hold you to your word without the grace to fit their answer to your meaning. Of all the secrets of worldly success or homely happiness, for ourselves or others, there is nothing like perfect sympathies. "There's such divinity doth hedge a king;" there's such a balmy influence sheds its halo around a really sympathetic soul. Some musical buildings deliver us of our voice, some sympathetic people of our thoughts and feelings, their heartstrings being in perfect tone and unison with our own. This is a character truly invaluable; and for its first growth and culture commend me to the society of Oxford. Even if I had learnt "small Latin and less Greek" I should still feel my academical days not wholly thrown away.

As to the chief studies of Oxford, what can be more valuable than to study man—human thought and human character—and to study man under such varieties of age and clime as shall distinguish between individual peculiarities and the caprices of fashion, and the creature man as his Creator made him? Some persons think geology preferable as a study; some would suggest astronomy, or chemistry, or any other science. I am myself much interested in the strata of the three series, nor do I look with indifference on the starry firmament above, or in organic formations below, but still I must maintain that "the proper study of mankind is man." The *nil admirari*—that knowledge of human nature which makes us surprised or disappointed at nothing, which enables us to identify every fault and foible, every virtue, vice, or passion, in many a scene and character in this world's drama, in an almost unbroken series from Adam to the present day—this claims precedence for youth over all other studies; and such are the chief studies of Oxford.

Some men examine curiously a Saxon coffin, or armour worn at Flodden Field, and boast a great discovery in inferring that the stature of man is at least as large as in former ages. With no less triumph do men pronounce on the structure of fish or plants anterior to the flood. And is it less curious, less a triumph, to penetrate and to analyse the thoughts and feelings of generations past; to ascertain that for thousands of years the heart of man has throbbed with the same emotions, that envy and other passions have borne the same torture to the breast; and that conscience in the days of Æschylus as well as Juvenal has shaken the same avenging scourge over the guilty head? I will conclude with a quotation worth considering in Mr. Stedman's excellent manual beforementioned :—

"The man of letters may view with admiration the monuments which the genius of Plato, Demosthenes, and Cicero have left to posterity; the orator may read with both pleasure and profit the models of eloquence; the student of war may follow with delight the campaigns of the most consummate strategists of all ages; the poet may turn to works which have never been surpassed; the historian to authors whose writings, now more than two thousand years old, are yet the choicest product of the historic muse. These books, read where the very atmosphere is classical, where every stone and tower speak of an antiquity which is perennial, of a learning which will survive the inventions of this modern age as it has survived the struggles of a thousand years— must not these invigorate the mind and chasten the spirit, and render the whole man fitter and more able to meet and conquer those trials and temptations which must necessarily beset him?"

Cardinal Newman says, in his own forcible but

simple style:— "A College is a home for the young who know nothing of the world and who would be forlorn and sad if thrown upon it. It is the refuge of helpless boyhood, which would be famished and pine away if it were not maintained by others. It is the providential shelter of the weak and inexperienced, who have still to learn how to cope with the temptations which lie outside of it. It is the place of training for those who have not yet learned how to learn, and who have to be taught by careful individual trial how to set about profiting by the lessons of a teacher. Moreover, it is the shrine of our best affections, the bosom of our fondest recollections, a spell upon our after life, a stay for the world-weary mind and soul, wherever we are cast, till the end comes."

CHAPTER XXX.

GETTING OUR SONS OFF OUR HANDS.

"Blessed is the man that hath his quiver full of them." This might have been very true of patriarchal days, each with a bow and arrow "when the enemy was at the gate;" but not so true of these hard times when "the wolf is at the door." A father who can afford a regiment of donkeys and nursery-maids for his babes, and hunters for the bigger boys, with savings enough from an entailed estate to make them all independent and comfortable in later days—this lucky man, perhaps, may feel proud and happy in his paternity; but where the family will grow and the income will not, and the father sees in his growing boys a sad vista of the same follies, foibles, and extravagances he so painfully remembers in his own younger days, he begins to feel a burden of dark cares and anxieties from which he must look about him to escape. This paternal difficulty is all the greater because no youngster ever realises the fact that his father's purse is exhaustible, and that all the little 'tis buts, which he seems a stingy old fogey to deny, amount, when multiplied, to a ruinous sum by the end of the year.

The wrong-headedness of youth is something distracting to a father, and not the less so when there is a grain of home-truth in their arguments. We remember one who, when told he must choose a profession and provide for himself, replied : " It's very hard. I never wanted to be born; and to bring a fellow *nolens volens* into an expensive world like this, with a big National Debt and an income-tax, and then to tell him you have not a screw to give him, is too bad a great deal." Another hardship the boy might have mentioned, we think, is that no man can as much as choose his own father or mother ; for it is on their discipline or indulgence that even the means of helping oneself so much depend. "Boys are spoilt for five years," said a crammer, "and then brought to me without any formed habits of application, to make up for lost time." No wonder many are disappointed, and the "kicks of life" come late, though "the halfpence" have been spent very early.

Well, perhaps it is in these said lines of competition that the supposed father first seeks to make one less around his crowded board. "Our soldiers swore terribly in Flanders," said Corporal Trim; but the family curses on the competitive system would outnumber all, though sworn perhaps in a more civilised way. The first remark we ever heard on this novelty was from an old lady of eighty years.

"O, dear! I am so sorry to hear it!"

"Why, mother?"

"Why, what's to become of all the stupid ones? and I am sure I have seen plenty of them."

Even as the barrow trade and the sandwichmen have been deemed a happy institution and resource where there is no character, so were the Government offices where there were no brains. But, for the good of the public service, all that is altered. Whereas the qualification used to be ignorance, now it is knowledge. The idlest and most useless son in the family was always the one reserved for some member of Parliament to prefer. It is easy to laugh at examinations, and to quote useless questions; but a remembrance even of useless facts in an examination is a test of industry and accuracy in reading; habits truly valuable in themselves when the studies that formed those habits are forgotten.

But good as this system is for the public service,

and good as a stimulus to education—for idle masters have nowadays their work brought to the test—and desirable also to the good and wise parents who are few, with clever sons who are fewer still, yet to the generality of families the pending examinations keep father and mother constantly on the fret with year after year of anxiety and misery. Go where we will, it seems as if fathers and mothers were at school again; their talk is of school histories, grammars and text books; and, worst of all, many a youth is tempted to compete without a chance of success, and only finds out his mistake when too late to begin in any other line. "Fond and foolish," as applied to parents, and "cruel kindness," are terms apt indeed. All life is self-denial, while its preparation in these days is too often self-indulgence. Live by labour is the law; a law from which few comparatively are in any sense exempt. Now, if parents would only look far ahead, and realise according to their child's powers of mind and body what his course in life should be, many a' heart-ache would be saved. *If;* yes *if* indeed! But man, though defined to be an "intellectual animal" in Buffon's *Natural History*, has too often the part of intellect left out, and is ruled by reason only as a rare exception. Hope, imagination, and "chancing it," are far more commonly the springs of human action; and as to forming an opinion of a son, no man knows so little of the son's character as his own father, though for the most part no one knows more of the father's weak side than his own son. The one is blinded by affection; the other is keen from tricks and habits of evasion, and sharp-set from the pleasure of the moment. Could the race of life be run like the donkey-race—each driving his neighbour's animal, each managing his neighbour's son—the result would be different indeed.

As it is, boys are trained and prepared for no one thing essential for life. The pocket-money they squander even in school-days is often far more than they will afford in later years. So to launch them into life—while wanting in self-command, in economy, or habits of industry and hard work, and to anticipate no danger of their soon falling back again on the family resources, is the hopeless attempt of many a foolish parent. As to success by competition for public appointments, though called so difficult, we well know that a youth, kept steadily at work, as boys used to be, for some five years at school, would with a short special preparation stand three-fourths up the list for anything but the Indian Civil Service and one or two other prizes, to compete for which, we admit, requires far more than average industry and talent.

Some who fail in examinations for a Commission we now see are sometimes so bold as to enlist. An amusing book lately published, entitled *Through the Ranks to a Commission*, will, however, show that the attempt is not one for an indulged and spoilt boy; and even when a Commission has been secured, the poor father finds it but a qualified advantage. An allowance is required, and with a small one, if he is not prepared to meet occasional demands, to save his son's honour, and his commission too, he must, indeed, calculate on exceptional sobriety and virtue amidst the temptations of the mess-room. Not off his hands still! We remember a poor subaltern telling us quite a heartrending tale, how once he was in dread of utter ruin simply because a Ball was voted, for which he had no money to subscribe. It was only by the self-denial of a very poor maiden aunt that the indispensable twenty pounds could be raised and his Commission saved.

Preferment by competition is, of course, all in favour of the steady and intellectual; but they are always a small minority. It is in vain to ridicule examinations, and argue that a good officer need not be a book-worm. No matter; you will find more good officers amongst those with wits than those without them; and as to saying that study far less than enough for a University degree will imply softness and effeminacy, every Cantab or Oxonian will laugh at it as absurd.

Some fathers hope their sons will make a fortune at the University, and depend on college scholarships leading as they do to fellowships, livings, head-masterships, and—for such are most common stepping-stones—even bishoprics. No doubt many a man, without a shilling beyond his University expenses, has mounted nearly all the steps aforesaid; only for this attempt two qualifications are essential—not only very superior talent, but very rare self-denial and inflexible perseverance. College-life has its distractions and most seductive diversions; and few live strictly within their allowance, whether great or small. One year's income in arrears at taking the degree is only a reasonable calculation. Those who realise the parental expectations of "making a fortune" at the Universities are a very small number. This reading "for the pot," and riding Pegasus for the stakes you can win; and wooing the Muses, not for their charms, but for their fortune, is indeed a very risky way to stop all drafts on the family bank.

We need say little of Law, or of Medicine, or of the Church, because we are speaking of getting clear of a son's expenses once and for all. Neither in Law nor in Medicine can any one commonly be floated without an allowance for several years; and as to the Church being a provision for a man, without unusual interest or good expectations most clergymen would have been richer if they had saved their educational expenses, and lived on the interest, while in the pursuit of something else. The high social advantages in the Church used to be deemed a great compensation; but in these days of Literates and ordained schoolmasters, the name of Reverend is not, without inquiry, the same passport to Society which it once was.

All these risks and difficulties are so apparent that parents of late years have generally come to the conclusion that professions are overstocked, and rarely pay; and therefore some boldly resolve that either trade or emigration—if they will only prefer the substance of worldly comforts to the shadows of gentility, and "what the world says"—presents at last the opening for which they are seeking for their sons.

This happy time, perhaps, may one day come;

but unfortunately we are at present yet in a transition state. Trade and commerce are growing genteel, but only growing still. The trade to be tolerated must be something on a large scale: it must be that of the wealthy merchant, not the struggling shopman; and as to the class of men of whom we are speaking, if they had money enough for the former they would prefer to be idle and spend it, and decline business altogether.

Brewing has been the snare of many. Some brewers have been called merchant princes, and are allied with noble families, whence the saying, "You may visit your brewer, but not your wine-merchant;" still their number is very small—"so few," said Mr. B., "I could count them on my fingers; and yet these few are such a bait as to cause us to be pestered to take the sons of our friends and neighbours, with a view to partnership, no doubt."

Dr. Johnson spoke of Thrale's brewery as "the potentiality of wealth beyond the dreams of avarice;" but on a small scale there is no business of more detail and drudgery or less likely to make desirable returns. Still, people easily believe what they wish to be true, and, in the way of a mild dose of trade, greet what seemed an eligible opportunity of combining the profits of the tradesman with the standing of the gentleman. "I can hire a man to stir up the malt for a pound a week," said Mr. A., "and that I should be sorry to give to any of these young gentlemen. If you try to live the life with the business of a brewer and of a gentleman too, believe me, you must fail."

"Well," says the anxious father, "what I propose seems reasonable; it is simply this: the money I might spend with small return at the University, or in articling my son to a solicitor, surely I can employ in buying a business or partnership in some house in Liverpool or in Mincing Lane."

My good friend, I am sorry to damp your hopes, but you are beginning at the wrong end. You think to begin at the top, but in all safe and profitable trade you must begin at the bottom—yes, and work very hard too for many a long year—quite in the spirit of Longfellow, when he wrote "Learn to labour and to wait." With a little reflection, can you believe that any safe and prosperous merchant will give you more than the ordinary interest of your money when you are utterly useless in business? A youth apprenticed for five years commonly works for four years for nothing, because all the time he is worth nothing, and is only deemed worth £100 for the fifth year. Even if you enter your son as an apprentice to learn his trade, at the end of the term the blanks of trade very greatly outnumber the prizes.

An experienced City wine-merchant, after forty years, told me that only about one in four of his friends had in any way succeeded. As to those who prove so valuable to their employers that they are promoted to places of £400 or £500 a year or a partnership, the employer of two hundred City clerks said that not one in a hundred proved worth more than £100 a year, though he was most desirous of selecting some fit for the higher places in his office to relieve himself—so rare are business habits and the peculiar talent that merchandise requires. The only chance of investing money for a son in business is to wait for proofs of high qualifications in the proposed business first; such men are always in demand. A merchant who would take your money under any other circumstances must be in a rather critical position, and the wrong man to intrust with your money or your son.

No doubt, among the large City dealers, where business has extended beyond the vigilance of any single man, the secret of success is in self-multiplication. But the man to replace the dealer's self and dispense with his labours to any extent must be a piece of human machinery of punctuality like clockwork, and with habits which imply a sacrifice of many a long year, without even any rational enjoyment and all that is worth living for. While men envy the position of a Maple or a Shoolbred, they little think of the toil and self-denial by which that eminence has been attained—a price at which they would be sorry, indeed, to purchase all such riches or renown.

We are afraid all this is very discouraging, but the question is, is it not true? Many of the class we address were, perhaps, born to fortunes; in other words, the hard work of life was done for them, and the wages of labour realised, and all made ready for their soft and luxurious reception in this, which is to the many a very hard world indeed. Some have a business well established, which their sons can keep going with comparatively little labour. And therefore, at the present day, a great social change is taking place. The men of labour are treading out the men of leisure. However proud men are of paternal acres which pay but little, those who deal in manufactures claim to be as genteel as those devoted to manures. And as to county influence and a long retinue of retainers at the poll, things which remind us of ancient feudal days, there is no such influence as the longer purse; no such willing slaves, no such homage paid as that which arises from the sight of the cotton thousands as compared with the landed hundreds, when the one can give a park to the people, while the other must mortgage his own! Truly, the county people are fast giving way to the count*er* people, and there are just now an unusual number of worn-out families—all spending and no earning from generation to generation having produced its natural results. Hence the cry, "Our sons must do something; the professions are full and overdone—where in the world shall the livelihood be found?"

To lose caste is as bad in England as in India; and here is the difficulty. The poor milliner might be in luxury as a servant; but "man doth not live by bread alone." Many would rather starve in stomach than in sensibilities. This feeling runs through all classes. "My father kept an hotel," said an old coachman; "and when I wanted to take to a coach, the difficulty which the family raised was this: if I demeaned myself to be a coachman, I could not be company for the cardroom, and gin-and-water every evening in the room behind the bar." Such feelings are falsely called pride; we call them what they are, natural

—in other words, Nature's own spur to industry; the voice with which she supports labour's primeval law, crying "Excelsior! Forward in the fray, and scorn to fall out of the ranks!"

To be a clerk in one of the joint-stock banks is a not unpleasant employment; but the pay is not much more than many a youth spends as pocket-money; and a very small proportion can possibly rise to be managers. "If you would know the value of money, try to make some," is a true saying. A man with capital and a knowledge of business combined has a great advantage; but it is a mistake to suppose that any one without this knowledge of business can ever find an opportunity of investment in the City, whether as principal or partner, which is not either a swindle or the road to ruin.

The conclusion of all this is that the advantages of trade are not for the sons of poor gentlemen, least of all while they retain the feelings and rank of gentlemen. Such feelings are a decided bar to success. Where the grocer's son feels rich and prosperous, the gentleman feels poor and disgusted. "To begin at the bottom, and work very hard," and to look for no probable results till youth and the years of enjoyment are passed, is the report of all old tradesmen.

In the greater houses of business in Liverpool and Manchester, as in the Stock Exchange and Mincing Lane, there have of late years been recognised not a few men of good birth and social standing. Some men for a season sink to rise; some sink lower still, and have enlisted and submitted to herd with the common soldiers, with prospect of a commission and resuming their proper status after three or four years of drudgery; but as to the position of a common shopman being endured by a gentleman, we never yet have heard an instance.

Nowadays emigration seems to many the point of escape. In a colony we can do things which we cannot do in England, and enjoy healthful work, fearing the frowns of no master. That "all business is imperious" is a well-known maxim, and most masters are imperious too; nor is there a greater drawback to a man's happiness than a constant feeling of nervousness about pleasing one set in authority over him, to say nothing of the liability, in any but a Government office, of being sent adrift at his caprice. Men who have roughed it in New Zealand have agreed that, if plenty of arm-ache, there is far less of heart-ache; and if plain food, a better appetite and health to enjoy it. Add to this, there is scope for our energies in a colony, and a hope of ultimate independence rarely to be earned in England.

But the question is, Is your son, both in body and in mind, suited for the life? The advantages of a colony may be stated briefly thus:

1. There is less competition; but you must have something of a kind wanted in a colony to compete with.

2. You are not ashamed to do things which you would not do at home; but that is no advantage unless you can do them.

"There is nothing for nothing in this world," least of all in a colony; and the something to be offered must be of a limited kind. Labour is the current coin—the labour either of your own hands, or the power to direct, and therefore multiply, the labour of others. As Falstaff said of wit, we say of labour: if none of your own, you must be "the cause of *labour* in other men." If you emigrate with only a little money in hand, you must be able to hew wood and clear bush, and do a better day's work than will commonly be so called at home. You must sell your labour first, and qualify to turn over your money afterwards. If you have capital, you may enter on sheep-farming, in which line you may fag less, but still no little; but here we must warn you that knowledge and tact are required. Thus in the beautiful climate of New Zealand you may find a sphere for many a gentleman; but as to the care of stock in a Canadian winter, this is suited to very few. Some have friends in a colony to join, and good friends lead to fortune everywhere; but this is exceptional, and not the common lot of colonists.

In a colony everything of the nature of office work and pen-and-ink work is both scarcer in itself and subject to more fierce competition than in England. Everything that a gentleman is best able to do, and, for the most part, the only stock-in-trade he carries with him, is there superfluous, and will not be in demand for a generation to come. A colony wants many hands, but few heads. All our experience—over fifty years of observation — proves that among gentlemen colonists, of those who trust to their own labour alone, the failures are very many, and the depths to which gentlemen may sink are often concealed, as too sad to be told at home. We once educated a youth as a surveyor and engineer, and we have the satisfaction of knowing that he carried the right goods to the right market. We have no doubt a skilful carpenter would generally keep himself from first landing, and sometimes turn contractor in a larger way. Amateur carpentering and turning will not do; and what gentleman will work for years to qualify himself in a carpenter's shop?

"But if you have capital?" Well, a colony offers a wide field for the capitalist; but capital wants judgment in all countries, and is lost as well as squandered, for sharpers are found quite equal to the occasion in a colony as at home. At the Canterbury settlement, for instance, you may invest safely at higher interest than in England; but interest is falling; capital is sent out to invest, and good securities from eight per cent have sunk to six. In a colony you should wait a year at least, and look about you, and, if the right man, you may find an opening in land or stock that may lead to riches. We may well say "if the right man," because give land and stock for nothing, and some men abroad as at home would lose money in farming.

If this view of life is not a very encouraging one, we can only say that, however sorry to be the bearer of ill-news, we cannot help it. The truth sooner or later must crop out; better to hear it before you burn your fingers than after. If born a gentlemen, it takes, at present prices and with the present habits of society, far more to keep you as a gentleman than most gentlemen can earn. Gentility goes out sighing in the money market in these days. Men do not in business pay money for nothing or make much allowance for sensitive feelings. With gentility you are heavily weighted—indeed, in the race for riches a gentleman and a do-nothing are convertible terms. A bishop in New Zealand some time since found it necessary to make a public address to combat a very mischievous opinion then widely prevalent in that colony, and to argue that a man was not to be presumed to be useless to an employer because he was a gentleman—there called "a swell."

The step from professions which are full to the rank of mechanics which still find a wide demand for their labour, we admit, is one painful indeed to take; but, sooner or later, there can be no alternative. Gentility cannot increase and multiply with any satisfactory result unless men do so in the spirit of the Psalmist, who, after saying "they have babes at their desire," also pre-supposes that we "leave the rest of our substance to our babes." We pity the poor babes born to none. The latter part is too often left out. As to going on from generation to generation, each poorer than the last, eating away at the family cake, yet still expecting to have it—this is a downward course which, without a periodical turn at reproduction, must end in disappointment at no distant day.

We once heard a gentleman say, "My grandfather drove four-in-hand, my father drove a pair, I can hardly afford a 'one-horse shay.' Happily, I am a single man; but suppose I married, and multiplied after my kind: some of my sons must come down to a wheelbarrow, and perhaps, by good luck and industry, rise to be railway contractors, and start the family coach, to run through the same gradations over again."

But it often occurs to us, What is to become of those lounging loafers whom we meet at every corner in—any fashionable resort? It is a mistake to say they do nothing. They earn nothing, or do no good, if you please. In sober truth, they do as much of a certain sort as some valuable members of society, only the latter spend little and do much; the former spend much and do nothing—but mischief. They smoke and nip sherry, play billiards or lawn-tennis, with flirting variations; they hang about young ladies and keep better men away, and are a heartache to their fathers and mothers, whom we only do not pity because they have themselves to blame for having animated such useless lumps of mortality. First of all they drain their parents, and leave less for their long-suffering sisters. Soon idleness leads to vice and scrapes various, that must be paid for—a sacrifice which the respectability of the family requires. The next stage is one of mature years. The father is dead, the income divided, of which the scamp has anticipated nearly all his share. His family have suffered enough, and he must look to himself. As to general society, that becomes impatient. Men say, "We would make allowance and entertain youths, but Mr. Dolittle is too old." He soon feels that he has arrived at the give-and-take age. There crops up an instinctive feeling that he cumbers the earth, and is not to be encouraged, and a social nuisance. It has long been too late for him to begin at anything. He is too ignorant and useless to be master, and too old and independent to be man. He may gamble, cheat, borrow, and not pay, or turn tout and want to order every one's wine and every one's coals.

Some years since we marked such a specimen in the earliest part of his downward course; he then had succeeded to some little money, but we predicted he one day would come to the ground, a prediction most painfully verified. We met him in Bath, not long since, all rags and tatters. He had turned billiard-marker, and been discharged; had been porter at a wagon-office; and, unfit for anything, we saw nothing before him but starvation or the workhouse. If such cases are not common, it is that some poor relative divides a crust with them, or not uncommonly because they avoid all the haunts of their former friends. However kindly disposed, you find it a difficulty to acknowledge them. You carry not "Cæsar and his fortunes," but your shabby-genteel relative and his vices.

Young men, be wise in time. In a few years all family supports, by the ruthless hand of Death, will be knocked from beneath you, and you will find yourself launched on the stormy seas of real life, to sink or swim, with no helm or buoyancy but your own. You will then learn too late the truth that, severed from his family circle, man has no friend but his money; or, if any, those only who are to be attracted by such virtues and amiable traits as no ruined spendthrift or idle loafer can ever be supposed to possess.

One word to fathers. Eton and Harrow, yes, and Winchester, with its motto, "Manners make the man," are true to this wise maxim, no doubt.

Many is the man who, from an unlicked cub, has emerged from these schools with a degree of taste and style valuable for social life. Admirable institutions to teach you to spend money gracefully, but the very worst to learn to earn any. One of our most economical friends said that he could not allow his son less than twenty-five pounds a year for game subscriptions and pocket-money. Granted that the outdoor in the school-life of boys is not to be neglected. A happy childhood supplies a fund of pleasing recollections for after-life; but the question is what you can afford, and whether the life in prospect for your son does not require hard work, economy, and self-denial. If the time for hard work must come, is it not wise to initiate him by degrees? There is no such cruel temptation as to place him among those far richer than himself, when want of money bids him skulk off and mope alone whenever any costly frolic is proposed. We now see boys with more sovereigns than they used to have half-crowns, and the whole system of modern education seems to anticipate a life of luxury and of ease; and yet such a lot is harder to earn than ever, and therefore when off their father's hands and on their own, sons will have little cause to thank parents for such disqualifying indulgence. No wonder we hear of hundreds of competitors for one situation — constabulary, office, or secretaryship—yes, and see not a few men driving hansom cabs whose voice and address painfully suggest that they have seen better days.

CHAPTER XXXI.

THE GOOD OLD TIMES—PAST AND PRESENT COMPARED.

Dr. Johnson said, "A traveller cannot at the same time drink of the mouth and of the source of the Nile;" and the nearer you approach the one the further you recede from the other. This is true of the "good old times" as compared with modern times. We are not about to deny our advantages, but simply to argue they are not unqualified. Former days had their own set of advantages too; and with all we have gained there is much we have left behind. Nor is it a slight consideration that our surroundings may alter, but not ourselves. Our pleasures may vary, but not increase. As a boy, we relished ginger-pop as much as when older we enjoyed champagne.

The question is one of comparison—how much on the balance we are the better or the happier, and how much life runs smoother and more pleasantly on the whole, for all the inventions and facilities of these last fifty years. There is a certain hullucination and excitement, and a certain harmony of feeling and equanimity, on which our happiness depends. Granted the result, it little matters how insignificant the means. *Quid refert dum felix sis?* " What's the odds while you're happy ? " says the schoolboy. " If a man is tickled with a straw, he only wants a straw given him to be tickled with." In other words, the means and elements of happiness are very simple : by multiplying your means you do not necessarily affect the result, for that depends less on the dainties than on the appetite, less on what the world calls pleasure than on a healthy moral nature to extract pleasure from it.

Still, we can imagine some one objecting, " See that picture of the old stage-coach. Ten miles an hour was deemed fast travelling. How often have we sat twelve hours between London and Bath—one of four on a seat like a knifeboard, amidst summer's heat or winter's frost and rain and snow, and the cost more than double of the express train ! "

Our reply is, Very true ; but then we seldom travelled ; we sought and found our resources nearer home. We had one expense the less ; for railway fares have become a necessary of life, one more family expense, and one more hardship added to our lot is to be unable to afford them. We have one more desire to gratify. Without being too philosophical, we may be allowed to ask if it were not better to be without the extra desire. Ask any paterfamilias, and see what he will say. But a great point is that in ante-railway days we lived with more composure, not so restless and given to change. One and the same set of neighbours more generally continued to surround us, whereas now, " man never continueth in one stay "—all is change, and families seem ever on the wing.

It may also be objected that we had no penny post, but eightpenny and tenpenny letters in those days. But then we were not always excited or nervous about the postman's knock—at most but once a day. Letters were few and far between. The extra fret and worry of our penny letters, circulars and all, does no little to keep up " life's fretful fever." The heart throbs all the faster, and, therefore, as Longfellow says, " beats funeral marches to the grave."

If we often are, at a friend's dictation, hurried off a hundred miles as a mere trifle—for some family wedding or to see the last new baby—we are equally far from remaining free agents as to hurry and flurry if the demand for a return of post reply gives more extra beats to the same vital organ. Shall anybody say that this is a slight matter—to live liable to have your pulse quickened at the caprice of any intrusive fellow who likes to write, and to have so much more vital force taken out of your system *nolens volens*? Shall any one say that this is not a great set-off against these modern facilities, however valuable when we really want them?

"But of the telegraph—wonders on wonders—what do you say?" We say the same, that there is nothing for nothing in this world—no rose without a thorn. There is a Nemesis in all these acknowledged blessings. Man's nervous system pays the smart, and that pay no little, for the convenience. A man's heart in these days has become like the dial of the said telegraph: he is at the mercy of any man at the end of any one of many hundred wires able, at his caprice, to send an electric shock to his system. All this makes us live too fast; the cares and brain work once spread over a week or a month come pulsing and throbbing and chasing each other in a single day. Life has lost no little of its old-time composure. The game of life is like short whist instead of long. Three events come off in the time for one. All is at high pressure and a breathless pace.

"The eternal worry of maid-servants," of which we hear so much, is only another result of our boasted facilities of locomotion. A girl no longer limited to your home circle, where her character might be known for good or for ill, reads her mistress's *Daily Telegraph,* picks out an advertisement, and gives sudden notice that, "to better herself," she has decided on a place just heard of some fifty miles off. All this independence of local ties, and of the opinion of those above them, cannot fail to be the loss of much moral influence, nor can all these facilities for the scattering of the people fail to render all government difficult, with a lawless and democratic effect on the national character.

But what will you say to our wondrous inventions—the extension of our manufactures—the cheapening of things both for the use and the elegances of life? Once more we answer, that though these things are acknowledged blessings, they are not blessings without alloy. The rural population is fast turning into a manufacturing and a town population, exchanging the fresh breezes of the country for the malaria of the streets; many a field being poisoned by the black smoke from these tall chimneys, and many a beautiful stream running foul or purple with the waters from the mill. These people, if richer at times and better clad, are they necessarily healthier or happier? Are they not far more than the rural population liable to sudden reverses and changes from demoralising plenty to the depths of poverty, because brisk trade tempts numbers of labourers, far too many in days of overtrading and of glut, to compete for the wages of the town?

It is painful to sit down and seriously to reflect on the consequences, present and to come, of this crowding into towns—no small offset to the glories of our commercial pride. Is it no drawback to our boasted inventions and division of labour that our machinery turns men into machines?—"the iron entering even into their souls"—as it condemns human beings with immortal souls to head pins all their life, or in many ways to form, as it were, one of a hundred cogs in the big wheel of Glasgow life! Is it nothing to stunt the bodies of men and cut short half their days in grinding forks or dipping phosphorous matches, and thus entailing an enfeebled physique from generation to generation? Nor is this all. Our overdone manufacturing system tends to increase the very population which it serves thus to degrade and degenerate. Marriages, say the Registrars, are promoted by two opposite causes. The first cause is great trading prosperity; because in such times people feel they can afford it. The second cause is a strike or turn off of hands; because then people are so miserable they think they cannot possibly do worse!

This festering town population, yearly on the increase, is indeed a price to pay for our commercial advantages. There you have thousands congregated together in a limited space, all on about the same dead level, owning neither respect nor allegiance to any superior, and strangers even to the very masters who employ them, and thus removed far from all feudal ties or from any one principle to elevate or civilise them. A London magistrate, knowing well the danger of such a lawless and uncontrollable mass—a brute power which you have only to see a Hyde Park meeting or even an illumination night to realise—said every day when he rose in the morning he felt it a mercy that London had not been sacked in the night.

There has been a sensible change in the health and constitution of men during the high pressure and express speed of this go-ahead generation. Witness the change of liquors; strong ale, bowls of punch, and port-wine are almost things of the past. Doctors tell us how by fast living the brain is exhausting the body, and it has become the fashion to trace our maladies to our nerve centres. No doubt the national constitution is sensibly affected. Perhaps we have not yet arrived at the hurry and flurry of life in America, where men bolt their dinner with knitted brows and excited brain, and off to business with the viands in their throats; but the same causes are fast betraying us into the same effects. The nervous temperament is predominating over the sanguineous, and we may say, in the spirit of Horace, to a nervous progeny will be transmitted the nerves of their sires. The Romans, in making an empire, unmade themselves, and the native vigour of barbarian hordes proved too much for an effete civilisation.

Another point on which men congratulate themselves in our commercial eminence is our banking and financial system. What if we had to keep and count out our money, to collect our own dividends, and to dispense with cheques and bills of exchange? With our existing arrangements, a few millions only of gold lie idle to give confidence in thousands of millions of commercial transactions. If payments were all in specie, some twenty railway wagons, it has been calculated, would be required to convey the gold that daily is represented by paper down Lombard Street;

whereas now, by exchange of balances at the clearing-house, the alteration of a few figures in the accounts of the respective bankers at the Bank of England settles all differences without a single sovereign passing. This saves the loss of interest on millions of gold, otherwise to be kept profitless for this single purpose. This also facilitates commerce to an extent of untold millions otherwise utterly impossible.

All very true; but, *per contra*, when Lord Overbury was once asked, with reference to this ingenious system, what kind of wreck and wholesale bankruptcy, with consequent starvation and riot in manufacturing districts, where thousands of labourers would be suddenly without wages, he would anticipate, if an enemy landed and held its ground one month in England, he replied, as incalculably ruinous and terrible beyond all conception, "It must not be!" Is it, then, no set-off to all these advantages to live as over a volcano? For, with all the bills, paper money, and bank credits daily existing as so many promises to pay, there exists not a hundredth part of the specie required to pay them, and our only safety is that any large proportion of creditors do not happen to want specie at the same time. London Bridge is wide enough when there is no sudden rush of panic-stricken thousands all at once. So our reserve of specie is big enough for quiet times; but there is not a merchant in London but would be insolvent if all London were rushing for payment in specie at the same time. We realise this even in a comparatively small way when there is a Black Friday in the City; the Bank of England wants relief, and houses otherwise prosperous, leaning one upon another, fall like a child's house of cards. Lord Macaulay wrote that, in the wars of Charles's time, an army marching through one farm left the neighbouring farms just as before; whereas, with the commercial combinations of these days, a war in England would be felt for years at the further corners of the globe. The truth is, we are no longer units, but links in one world-encircling commercial chain; and millions find that the conditions of modern life expose their nervous system to the liability of shocks peculiar to these advanced and supposed preeminently happy days. Here again, we are not denying our advantages; we are only contending that, if we have them, we pay for them, and enjoy (if we do enjoy) the blessings of this generation by a sacrifice of the calm composure of the generation past. Thousands live with knitted brows and racking brains; and, while a savage will face death unmoved, the City man turns pale at a fall of one per cent.

All these facilities are also snares. "Riches" nowadays may truly be said to have "wings"— paper wings—with which, too, the modern Icarus is ever threatened with a collapse. Civilisation is very hard on some of these gentlemen. Many a man who now loses his head among acceptances, scrip, and *omnium*, would have been quite able to manage Job's estate in flocks and herds, and would have been kept out of difficulties. We once sent a spendthrift to a colony, with good results. He no longer ran in debt, because no one would trust him, and his small stock of prudence proved equal to this primitive state of things. It is hard to rob you of acres of land, or to drive off more than part of a flock of sheep; but your agent, with shares and coupons, may be off to America with all your fortune in his pocket, or perhaps cheat you of it by the scratch of your pen.

Adam Smith said that this world was not in favour of men of sanguine temperament. An Irishman enjoys what he calls his hundred a year, though "faith, it is only for one year;" but a Scotchman would have no appetite for the dinner of to-day if he doubted dinners ahead for many a year to come. The ups and downs of life and sudden reverses multiply in the ratio of our national prosperity. The more trade, the more bankrupts, and a failure at the Antipodes shuts up mansions in Belgravia. Feelings of anxiety and uncertainty, and a severe fretting of the nerves at all times, if not a jar on our very heartstrings, are what we pay for being born in this luxurious generation.

Again, we do not deny the treasures of our libraries, nor the world-wide collections of the daily press. We wish not the sun of civilisation to go back upon the dial; but are we the happier or the wiser for it? At least, were our tastes or our intellects ungratified before? Certainly not. The mind, like the mill, can only convert a certain quantity, and is burdened and clogged with excess. Hobbes said, "If I had read as many books as some other men, I should know as little." And Southey, in the library of the British Museum, exclaimed, "Had I studied in this place, I should have been too distracted by all this literary wealth to bring any one subject to perfection."

Men exclaim, "These are prosperous times," and seem to pity those who lived in a less luxurious and wealthy age. They forget that wealth is relative, and that to all but the destitute, and those without "food and raiment" enough "to be content," wealth is chiefly the field in which men compete and rival each other for social position; and when all are equally enriched, the result so far is the same. The weekly list of wills proved shows how much richer men die nowadays, but not how much happier they live. "A rich man," said Adam Smith, "is only a large distributor;" and he might have added, he cannot be free from the harassing or the jealousies of this distribution.

A costly establishment, with elegant furniture and dashing equipages, cannot but be an addition to our cares and anxieties if we take any interest in them, and of only nominal value if we feel none. Many a rich man is a slave to his own servants when they outnumber his family out of all proportion. One of a dozen servants once was heard to say, "This is our establishment, and master and mistress are our housekeepers." The larger the fortune spent, the greater the load of life—very low life too—with which you must encumber yourself. Charles V. was one of very few who ever abdicated a throne; but thousands have retired from high positions, and ended their days in retirement, feeling, "Miserable comforters are you all." And since all that adds to the elegance and splendour of our houses widens the gulf between the dainty habits of the mansion and the dirt of the cottages, in which alone our servants can be reared, no wonder that the cry about inefficient servants is daily louder and louder, when everybody is richer, everybody wants more servants, till the stock of good servants is exhausted. When the cream is gone you come to the skim-milk. The master finds he has daily less control: the supply dictates to the demand. Servants engage masters and mistresses quite as truly as the latter engage them, and the result of the boasted riches of the day is simply this—that you keep open house for the lower orders, of a class daily more and more independent and useless.

A hundred years ago wine was rarely introduced at table; fifty years ago, chiefly the cheaper wines were expected; now champagne is everywhere. But has society become more pleasant with these causes of expense? No; society is more trouble and more fatiguing to the hosts, and therefore many enjoy less of it, while others crowd their rooms, making one party serve for two or three, a mere pretence at "a return"—too truly a "meeting of creditors"—the hostess but too happy when her friends are gone!

For luxury and superfluities of all kinds we do penance. "Pleasure," says Shakespeare, "with repetition souring, turns to pain!" All pleasure is no pleasure, and all holidays no holiday. This is too trite and obvious; but what seems not so obvious is that man cannot live by proxy. Nature cries "Work;" and inexorably does she avenge her broken law. We must either rub out or rust out. What we spare in aching limbs we suffer in a sinking heart. "My daughters want tonics," said a lady to Sir C. Clarke. "Yes, ma'am. Nature's tonic—work." Idleness, an aimless life, and *ennui*, Nature avenges on the nervous system. Our many servants, if called blessings, are a curse. Ladies wanted little of doctors' tonics in old-fashioned times, when they worked with servants "under them."—"But it is not the fashion."—"No not the fashion to be healthy—no fault of mine," replied the doctor.

We are creatures of a twofold nature, a two-stringed lyre, and the mistake is in harping upon one string. Our happiness, to use the terms of Bishop Butler, depends on two things: the satisfaction of active habits and the excitement felt from passive impressions; that is, impressions from without, when we are acted on, as distinguished from the said activities where our powers are called into action. Here we have a life of usefulness on the one hand and a life of pleasure on the other. But nineteen parts in twenty of the satisfaction of life consist in our said activities: their sphere is unlimited, for our facilities and sense of progress become ever greater and greater from exercise. But as to a life of impressions, of exciting pleasures of all kinds, our capacity for this kind of enjoyment is not only very limited, but it becomes less and less on repetition. The appetite is satiated, and luxuries sicken. Such pleasures lose their powers to please from exhaustion or deadened feelings. The human lyre is out of tune, and there is no response from within. Nor is there any state more pitiable than that of the effete, worn-out man of pleasure. This is the penalty he pays for seeking the nineteen parts of his pleasure where, from the very constitution of his nature, only the one-twentieth part is to be found.

Now, every one would wish to be rich, and regards a child born to a fortune as very favourably situated in life. But here again our blessings are by no means unqualified, because riches—we mean if more than moderate—can with difficulty be enjoyed without destroying the very balance we have just explained. The nineteen parts are sacrificed to the one, if, indeed, that one part of pleasure does not turn to pain. The happiest state to which life admits is that of a man who has a constant occupation and interest in his calling. The late Lord Derby, in a lecture, said: "Every man who lives an aimless, useless life is miserable, and deserves to be so." Riches make a man, in a common phrase, his own master; but he is too indulgent a master. We commonly want necessity, if not as a stimulus, at least to decide our choice. Labour, as we said, is Nature's tonic, and the very condition of our well-being. The rich man must labour to get an appetite for his dinner, the poor man to get a dinner for his appetite. Railways enable and tempt us to rush about, north, south, east, and west, for change—that is, in search of happiness; though, as Horace said, "it is as much at home as at Ulubræ. No man can run away from himself. They change the air, but not themselves, who fly beyond the sea."

And the same may be said of all the inventions and improvements of the last fifty years. Men had all the means and implements of happiness before; and, save the labourer, who is warmer and better fed, men now have simply a more distracting choice of means, the degree of happiness of which they are capable remaining just the same. There is one, and one only, kind of improvement by which we can really be affected: namely, the social, the moral, and, in the truest sense, the

Christian state of those around us—where envy, hatred, and all unkindness are little known, and we enjoy the calm serenity of a sphere of charity and loving-kindness.

THE END.

KELLY AND CO., PRINTERS, GATE STREET, LINCOLN'S INN FIELDS, W.C., AND MIDDLE MILL, KINGSTON-ON-THAMES.

www.ingramcontent.com/pod-product-compliance
Lightning Source LLC
Chambersburg PA
CBHW030815230426
43667CB00008B/1224